From the Impossible Burger and Beyond Meat to MorningStar Farms, Boca Burgers, and more, plant-based meats are a growing trend for those who want to help the planet, animals, and their health but don't want to give up the meaty flavors they love. In *The Vegan Meat Cookbook*, bestselling author Miyoko Schinner guides you through the maze of products available on store shelves and offers straightforward guidance on how to best use them in everything from Sausage Calzones with Roasted Fennel and Preserved Lemon to Hominy and Carne Asada Enchiladas with Creamy Green Sauce. Dig in to a satisfying vegan meal of Weeknight Shepherd's Pie with Bratwurst and Buttery Potatoes or Meaty, Smoky Chili. Wow your guests with Coq au Vin, Linguine with Lemon-Garlic Scallops and Herbs, or Lettuce Wraps with Spicy Garlic Prawns.

For those interested in making their own vegan meats and cheese from scratch, there are recipes for Juicy Chicken, King Trumpet Mushroom Bacon, Easy Buffalo Mozzarella, Miyoko's famous Unturkey, and many more that you'll never find in stores. Whether you're cutting back on meat for your health, the environment, animal welfare, or affordability, *The Vegan Meat Cookbook* will satisfy the cravings of flexitarians, vegans, vegetarians, and even carnivores.

THE
Vegan
MEAT
COOKBOOK

Meatless Favorites. Made with Plants.

Miyoko Schinner

Photographs by Eva Kolenko

TEN SPEED PRESS
California | New York

CONTENTS

Introduction

It may seem a bit strange that I would be writing a book on meat, even if made from plants. While I've earned the moniker "Queen of Vegan Cheese," my actual experience in eating meat is limited, having become a vegetarian at the age of twelve. Even before then, I had only eaten meat regularly for a few short years between the age of six, when I left Japan, and twelve, when I became a vegetarian. Prior to the year my mother and I emigrated from Japan to the United States, meat was an occasional treat. Here in the United States, however, my father made sure I got the best nutrition possible, which, to him, meant feeding me meat three times a day. I did get hooked on meat, and cheese as well—although *that* addiction lasted into my twenties.

When I stopped eating meat after a camping trip in middle school, kids at school would taunt me by shoving burgers in my face. It didn't bother me—nor did it tempt me. My desire for meat had disappeared overnight, and I no longer equated it with food. Meat was now recognized as an animal, someone who wanted to live as much as I did. No more would I want to eat a steak than I would want to eat a chair. I didn't struggle to stay vegetarian. It was easy.

However, my experience is unique. Most people don't make such transitions easily. We are all creatures of habit and culture, as we have been throughout history. We eat what everyone else eats, and that food helps to define our identity, who we are, to which community we belong. We want to eat familiar foods, go out for pizza with friends, or dig into a basket of fried chicken with our kids. So even if your vegan daughter or best friend tells you to go vegan to save the planet or animals, it's not often easy to do.

I was shocked to read that in 2018 meat consumption in the United States rose to an all-new high of 222 pounds per person. Americans have always eaten more meat than other populations, but the average person today consumes more than double what they did between 1900 and the 1950s (when the advent of TV dinners and fast food made eating meat not only fashionable but truly fun). Compare this statistic to many African countries where meat consumption is still less than 20 pounds per capita annually, or even in China where meat consumption has risen from 11 pounds at the turn of the twentieth century to over 130 pounds today. As meat consumption continues to soar in the United States and China, a third of Brits claim to have stopped or reduced eating meat altogether, and worldwide, according to Google, the word "vegan" is one of the top search terms. Even in the United States, over 50 percent of those polled cite an interest in reducing their meat consumption due to health, environmental, and animal welfare concerns. The center of the plate is in flux worldwide, and experts and people everywhere are discussing the future of protein. Where should it come from? Should it continue to come from animals who are "sustainably grown" and "humanely harvested," as if using euphemisms to equate animals with plants makes it better for the animal? Or should we invest in research in newer, novel proteins, such as insects or yeast? Is it simply an issue of needing to produce enough protein—any protein—to meet the needs of the world's exploding population? However much we try to deflect the issue by referring to it as simply a problem of protein sources, the reality is that what the world has an appetite for is *meat*.

We know that the planet cannot support the billions of livestock we force into the food system. We also know that it's cruel beyond words. At the same time, we can't forget the importance of the culture of food. We can't expect culturally indoctrinated populations to change their habits overnight. We must find solutions to help people transition—and those solutions have to be *delicious*. It's not just about nutrients, it's about taste and culture. We must remember that food needs to comfort people, provide joy, and create community. And at this point in human history, that means finding ways to supplant meat with viable plant-based alternatives.

Entrepreneurs and businesses across the globe are addressing the problem of how we feed 10 billion people by 2050 and not destroy the planet. The problem of climate change and food security isn't just for industry to solve; it is the business of each of us as consumers. We are actually more powerful than we realize, and our food choices can help redirect how we end up. Luckily, we are entering a time when there is exponential growth of "meat" that doesn't come from animals. These new offerings have made it easier for the meat-loving population to take environmental advocacy into their own kitchens. By the time this book is published, another dozen or more companies will have launched "meat" made from plants, providing even more options for you to explore. In addition to the myriad burgers and nuggets out there, there will be pork, steak, fish, and even lobster made from every possible seed, legume, and grain conceivable. There might even be some of the so-called cell-based meats that reside in the murky waters of confused identity—are they vegan or vegetarian if made from animal cells? Just as the dairy aisle has changed in composition from bovine milk to almond and coconut, the meat department could look like a very different place indeed if these products succeed in migrating from the produce section or frozen aisle.

Indeed, meat alternatives or "substitutes" are nothing new. They have been around for hundreds of years in Asia where Buddhist monks developed chewy substances from wheat and soy in order satisfy those earthly cravings that didn't go away despite hours of meditation. Go to any vegan Chinese restaurant, and you will be amazed by the multiple offerings that resemble duck, pork, beef, or even shark's fin, most of which are utterly delectable. In Vietnam, I had "pork" that was so spectacularly juicy and tender that I couldn't stop thinking about it all night. Even in the United States, companies such as Loma Linda have been making meat alternatives for decades. So, if that is the case, why is it only recently that the world has taken notice?

Hidden gems made from tofu or seitan at Asian restaurants may have excited an intrepid food explorer, but until recently, vegan options on grocery shelves simply weren't sexy enough to attract more than the strictest vegetarian. But rapid advancements in food technology from stalwart companies such as Tofurky and Gardein to newer, much celebrated ones like Impossible and Beyond Meat have landed plant-based meat on the map, and the world is clamoring for more. Even Tyson, Nestlé, Maple Leaf, and other traditional meat companies have gotten into the game, launching plant-based meat alternatives and investing in cutting-edge start-ups in the space. Products that were once tucked away only in a dark corner of health food stores are now proudly displayed at major grocery chains across the country, and even fast food chains are pushing plant-based alternatives with resounding success.

Who is buying these products? Studies show that the majority of consumers of plant-based meat are not vegan nor even vegetarian, but "flexitarian," representing the growing population of people that are trying to eat healthier by lessening the amount of animal products they consume. Other studies show that millennial and younger generations make purchasing decisions very differently from their parents and grandparents, considering the health, environmental, and ethical (both in terms of animal welfare and treatment of workers) impacts of the products they buy. With more information flooding the Internet about the disastrous environmental impacts of animal agriculture, combined with the unnecessary suffering of animals, it is no surprise that people would gravitate toward plant-based options.

However, one of the criticisms of some plant-based or vegan products is that they are too highly processed. While the traditional "meats" of Asia were relatively unprocessed (after all, monks made them in sparsely equipped kitchens with few ingredients), many of the products available today have mysterious, often unpronounceable ingredients, leaving some people questioning how truly healthy or "natural" they are. Even some strict vegans eschew plant-based meats for these reasons. In many ways, I would agree that some of the commercially available items are not the healthiest things you could put into your mouth—if you want to eat strictly for health, try kale. Or beans. Or strawberries. Or brown rice. But I would argue that they are still better than eating the cholesterol-and-hormone-laden flesh of a dead animal (at this point, there is too much science to support the unhealthfulness of animal products) and certainly satisfy a craving that one could say is good for the soul.

While selecting foods based on reasons of health is of high importance, in my opinion, we are at a critical point in history when we must think beyond our individual health to consider that of the planet *and* animals, both domestic and wild. The Amazon is burning, with 91 percent of the fires started to clear land for cattle grazing or to support livestock operations, and climate change is becoming more serious daily. Animal agriculture takes up almost half of all landmass in the United States; we simply do not have enough land, water, or resources to feed the growing population with meat, eggs, and dairy. Yes, human health is of utmost importance, but being healthy is meaningless if the world crumbles around us, along with billions of other nonhuman animals who played no part in causing the disaster of climate change. We have reached a point when we, as individuals, must assume some responsibility in making lifestyle changes that will mitigate and possibly even reverse climate change, save animals, *and* improve our own health. But the exciting thing is that we can do that without sacrificing flavor or texture or the satisfaction of something hearty, chewy, succulent, and delicious. We have now, on the world stage, magnificent alternatives to meat that are made with environmental and ethical standards. And if you don't like the ones on store shelves now, make some of your own—this book is filled with recipes for doing just that! Or just wait a few months, because I bet there will be many more showing up on store shelves.

This book features meaty recipes that utilize many of the new options in the marketplace. Some readers may have been vegan so long they forgot how to cook with meat, while those just exploring or experimenting with plant-based meats may find that they don't perform exactly like their animal counterpart and end up frustrated. It's true; many of them perform differently. While meat adds flavor to dishes, many meat substitutes are more or less inert, not oozing any juices (except a few of the "raw" type sausages, such as Beyond Sausage), fall apart if stewed for much longer than a few minutes, or simply lack umami. While they've indeed come a long way, some can use a little tenderness and love, or a little something to boost the flavor and deliver satisfying results. For example, vegan chicken breasts can be rather dry and tasteless, but if made confit-style by roasting them at low temperature in a bath of butter and wine, they become amazingly succulent and delicious.

For those who balk at the processed nature of the commercial meat alternatives but still want something to chew on, one chapter is devoted to making your own. Some of those recipes contain wheat or soy in creating traditional "wheat meat" or seitan, while others explore the wonderful world of meaty fungi. There are even innovative recipes transforming a medley of gluten-free legumes and grains to produce meaty staples for your kitchen. And, of course, most of these can be used in the recipes in the preceding chapters.

As a vegan of almost thirty-five years, I am happiest just feasting on veggies and rice (really—I eat very simply!). But at times, nothing short of a delicious meaty concoction will do. People often ask why a vegan or vegetarian would want to eat fake meat, but the truth is that we just want something substantive that's chewy, tasty, and succulent. I don't think most people—vegan or even omnivore—care if it tastes exactly like meat; we just want something to bite into with a lot of flavor. I hope that this book will satisfy that craving, whether it be for the latest and greatest commercial alternative or a juicy "chicken" made from mushrooms whipped up in your kitchen. And with culinary prowess, we can save the world!

A Commercial Meat Alternatives Primer

Between the time I write this book and its publication, many more meat alternatives will have hit store shelves, so the list that follows on pages 10–15 is by no means comprehensive (it's also possible that some of them will have been discontinued or never succeeded in taking off beyond a local market). While Beyond Meat and Impossible Foods have led the pack and made plant-based meats comprehensible and accessible to a greater population, there are a number of other players whose products are standouts as well. But let's be honest: Not all meat alternatives are great. Whether in the realm of vegan chicken strips or vegan ground beef, the flavor, texture, and quality can vary radically, so it is hard to generalize about all of them. As companies strive to innovate, all products will continue to improve as they have over the last decade, and we'll see major advancements in the next few years.

For the home cook, however, a tweaking of seasonings and cooking methods can help overcome flaws in some products, making them more universally acceptable. The recipes in this book are designed to work with many of the brands and compensate where the product is lacking with unique preparation or flavor adjustments.

Also, it's important to note that we'll be focusing on meat alternatives that are designed to be incorporated into recipes, rather than fully prepared ones, such as a fish fry that is already breaded and fried and just needs to be reheated. In other words, the products we're focusing on are those that can be an ingredient in a creative recipe, not just something to eat on its own.

Until recently, most meat alternatives were fully seasoned and ready to eat, the equivalent of fully cooked and seasoned meat, such as teriyaki-flavored seitan. For example, what was "ground beef" were fully cooked and seasoned "crumbles" that could be thrown into a dish at the last minute, or even eaten straight out of the package. Now, however, there are "raw" type products, first launched by Beyond Meat and followed by many other brands, that start out looking pink like their animal counterparts and then turn brown upon cooking. These are designed to be incorporated into foods in much the same way as foods of animal origin and require heat in order to be

Benevolent Butchers

Whether in Canada, Germany, or the United States, there is a growing trend of vegan butchers turning plants into meat and selling it by the pound from deli cases piled high with charcuterie of every sort. With names such as Herbivorous Butcher, YamChops, and the Butcher's Son, these shops offer locals the opportunity to purchase freshly made "beef," "chicken," "chops," and more in a fun, nostalgic atmosphere. Walking into YamChops in Toronto, I was tempted to try every type of sausage and barbecue seitan they had. In Minneapolis for a business meeting, I made sure to stop by the Herbivorous Butcher, where I had a steak au jus sandwich and took home some Korean barbecue, tucked away in my suitcase. In my own area, a visit to the East Bay often includes dropping into the Butcher's Son, one of the most popular spots in Berkeley (you'll notice that there is always a line out the door while nearby restaurants are empty). Then there's Cena Vegan, a food-truck-turned-retail product (see Plant Ranch, page 14), that has by far the best seitan crafted for tacos, burritos, and Mexican food. I remember my first visit there the line was two blocks long—meanwhile, a taco truck serving meat right next to it had nobody in line.

This is the wave of the future. As retail products expand, so will local vegan "butcher" shops bringing savory, fresh options with fun and flair.

Vegan Dairy Products

For the purposes of the recipes in this book, there are some dairy equivalents that I've recommended and others that I have not. There are so many really good nondairy milks out there that I've left it up to you to find a brand you like, except in some recipes where something like oat milk would be better than almond. For vegan cheese, I've made a few recommendations based on what I feel are the better brands, but for butter, I've been bold enough to toot my own horn (even though my mother would have been ashamed of me doing so) and only recommend Miyoko's. Why? It's because I feel it is simply the best, both for flavor and performance. It doesn't just prevent things from sticking but actually enhances the flavor of whatever you're cooking. Of course, you are free to choose another butter alternative, but all of the recipes in this book were tested with Miyoko's European Style Cultured Vegan Butter.

edible. Beyond Sausage is perhaps the most famous and successful of this type—it is a mushy, quite inedible product out of the package, but transforms into a chewy, hearty, savory sausage that oozes flavor and fat upon cooking. These products make for the easiest transition of traditional meat recipes to vegan ones.

It's also important to note that while similarities in ingredients exist for many of the products, such as wheat gluten, pea protein, and soy protein, some are less processed or have more whole foods–based ingredients. While many contain gluten, Beyond Meat relies on pea protein and does not, making it a great choice for those who are gluten intolerant. Moreover, some products have an ingredient list a paragraph long, while others are made with just a few simple things, such as whole soybeans, oil, and salt, or wheat gluten and water. It is up to you what type is most appealing and applicable to your situation. I am not here to dictate which are healthiest or cleanest—I leave the judgment to you. What I provide are alternatives to use in recipes that have been carefully crafted to work with a wide range of meat alternatives.

As there is such a wide variety of products with different flavors, ingredients, and accessibility, it's not as easy as simply calling for "beef" or "chicken" as in a dish using the animal version. Here, your personal preference, which may include dietary restrictions such as allergies toward a certain ingredient, come into play, as well as what's available to you locally or online. Therefore, while I may list some suggestions for a recipe, please note that they do not preclude other products that are similar—or will be in existence by the time this book is published! For many recipes, a homemade version of the meat alternative can be found in the Just Make It chapter, which presents more than two dozen versions of DIY meat and seafood.

It's a new age indeed, and a new wave of alternatives are just on the horizon. But for now, let's explore what's currently in the retail marketplace. Distribution for these products is also increasing with stores, both brick and mortar and online, expanding their selections all the time. With consumer shopping habits transitioning online more and more, many of the newer brands are focusing on e-commerce sales, and we'll see the major brands joining them in increasing numbers. Right now, Amazon and VeganEssentials.com are two of the best places to get the widest variety of meat alternatives, although you may have to pay a hefty sum for shipping.

ABBOT'S BUTCHER

Vegan Chicken, Beef, and Chorizo

abbotsbutcher.com

Started at farmers' markets in Southern California, Abbot's Butcher quickly gained popularity. Their website, along with their products, give a nod to the traditional butcher in look and feel. Their current lineup of three products—ground beef, ground chicken, and chorizo—are based on pea protein and wheat gluten, although their chorizo contains no wheat and is therefore gluten-free. They are an up-and-coming player on the scene—I look forward to seeing further developments from them. The flavor is fairly neutral, making it adaptable to many recipes. You can find their products online, as well as at independent natural food retailers.

ALPHA FOODS

Vegan Chicken and Beef

alphaplantbased.com

A new player on the scene that first launched with pocket pies and other convenience foods, Alpha Foods has vegan crumbles and chicken strips made of soy and wheat. The flavor for this brand is fairly mainstream and approachable, and their distribution is mainstream as well. You can find them at Safeway, Costco, and other large retailers.

BE LEAF

Vegan Chicken, Steak, Ham, Seafood, and More

beleafvegan.com

Be Leaf is a spin-off of a Taiwanese company that has been producing meat alternatives for years. Their product line is extensive, although their retail distribution in the United States as of this writing is not (they appear to be mostly food service). Half-chickens, steak, drumsticks, ham, seafood, and more can be found through their own store as well as at VeganEssentials.com. Most of their products are soy- and wheat-based with other interesting additions, such as mushrooms and fungi.

BETTER CHEW

Vegan Shredded Steak, Chicken, Fried Chicken

somethingbetterfoods.com

An up-and-coming start-up founded by Chef Chew, this frozen vegan meat company has a unique approach to making beef and chicken from soy that has a texture like none other. The product uses the whole soybean, not isolates or extracted proteins. It is available nationwide online and is gaining distribution through Whole Foods. At the time of this writing, they were primarily available at Whole Foods locations in Northern California and Las Vegas.

Pour the oil into a deep fryer, wok, or pot to a depth of 2 inches and heat over medium-high heat to 375°F. Now dip the coated konnyaku pieces in the flaxseed "egg," then coat them again in the flour mixture. Fry the pieces in the oil, being careful not to crowd the pan, until they are golden brown, 2 to 3 minutes. Drain on paper towels.

Serve with lemon wedges.

Variation

Gluten-Free Calamari Fritti: Use 1 cup rice flour, or ¾ cup rice flour and ¼ cup cornmeal, in place of the flour or semolina.

Pork, Green Onion, and Shiitake Pot Stickers

Makes about 30

Explore your inner dim sum with these delicious pot stickers made with Chinese Tender Pork. Pan-fried and steamed, or simmered in broth, these tasty morsels are fun appetizers or can be the entrée of an Asian-style meal.

8 ounces store-bought vegan pork, such as Hungry Planet, or homemade Chinese Tender Pork (page 198), diced

2 cups sliced green onions (white and green parts), about 2 bunches

4 ounces fresh shiitake mushrooms (2 cups), stems removed, diced

About ½ cup water

2 cloves garlic, minced

2 teaspoons soy sauce or tamari, plus more for serving

1 teaspoon toasted sesame oil

30 to 35 vegan pot sticker wrappers

2 tablespoons neutral oil, such as sunflower, canola, avocado or grapeseed

Chili oil and Chinese black vinegar (see Glossary) for serving

In a bowl, combine the pork and green onions. Put the shiitake mushrooms in a skillet, add 2 to 3 tablespoons of the water, and quickly steam-sauté over medium-high heat until the water has evaporated and the mushrooms are silky and tender. Add the mushrooms to the bowl and mix in the garlic, soy sauce, and sesame oil.

Now form the pot stickers: Prepare a small bowl of water for dabbing water with your finger. Take a wrapper and put about 2 teaspoons of the filling in the middle. Moisten your finger with the water and dab the perimeter of half of the wrapper. Fold over the wrapper to meet the other side and squeeze together. Quickly gather the sides together, folding and forming little pleats to keep the insides intact. Set aside on a dry plate or sheet pan. Repeat with the remaining filling and wrappers.

To cook the pot stickers, heat a large skillet with a lid over medium-low heat and add the oil. Place the pot stickers neatly in the pan, overlapping ever so lightly. Cook until the bottom is browned, 4 to 5 minutes. Now pour about ¼ cup of the water into the pan and cover immediately to allow them to steam for about 3 minutes, until the dough looks glossy and moist. The steam is what will cook the dough—pasta, essentially, which needs water or steam. Test a corner for doneness—if it seems tough, add a bit more water and steam for another minute or two until tender.

Serve with soy sauce, a little chili oil, and a splash of Chinese black vinegar.

Variation

Wonton Soup (serves 4): Instead of cooking the dumplings in a skillet, bring 3 to 4 cups of broth to a simmer. Add about 1 teaspoon soy sauce and a few slices of fresh ginger and simmer the pot stickers in it for 3 to 4 minutes. Add 2 cups tender leafy greens, such as spinach or Chinese broccoli, and continue to simmer for another minute, or until the greens have wilted. Stir in some sliced green onions and several drops of toasted sesame oil and serve.

Chilled Sesame Soba Salad with Chicken

Serves 4 to 6

The Japanese love to combine flavors and ideas of the West—such as salad, a thing unknown in Japan until the last few decades—with Japanese ingredients, so a salad of soba noodles with veggies and a bit of some protein is a natural for them. This can marinate for hours and be enjoyed for a potluck or picnic, as a main meal, appetizer, or side salad. While soba or buckwheat noodles are traditional, feel free to use leftover spaghetti. If you can find vegan crab, use it for an even more exotic experience.

SALAD

6 ounces buckwheat soba or other noodles (about 2 generous cups cooked)

1 tablespoon neutral oil, such as sunflower, canola, avocado, or grapeseed

8 to 10 ounces store-bought vegan chicken, such as The Better Chew, Tofurky, Gardein, or Plant Ranch; or homemade Juicy Chicken (page 210) or Savory Roasted Chicken (page 212); or store-bought vegan crab, thinly sliced

1 cup fresh or frozen shelled edamame

1 cup snow peas or sugar snap peas

2 cups packed shredded or julienned kale or collard greens

1 bunch green onions (white and green parts), thinly sliced

1 large carrot, grated

¼ cup black sesame seeds

DRESSING

½ cup white sesame seeds

½ cup neutral oil, such as sunflower, canola, avocado, or grapeseed

¼ cup soy sauce or tamari

3 tablespoons rice vinegar

3 tablespoons toasted sesame oil

2 tablespoons mirin (see Glossary)

2 tablespoons maple syrup

Make the salad: Cook the noodles according to package instructions. Drain well and run under cold water to cool. Cut the noodles roughly so they are approximately 6 inches in length—there is no need to do this precisely at all. Just bunch them up on a cutting board and cut them two or three times. Put them in a large salad bowl.

While the noodles are cooking, heat the oil in a nonstick skillet over medium heat and cook the chicken until browned, which could take anywhere from 2 to 5 minutes, depending on the brand. Put them in the bowl along with the noodles.

Put the edamame in the now empty pot, cover with water, and bring to a boil. Cook for 2 to 3 minutes. Add the snow peas and cook for another 30 seconds, then drain and cool under running water. Put the edamame and peas in the bowl with the noodles. Add the kale, green onions, and carrot to the bowl.

In the skillet, toast the black sesame seeds over medium heat until they start to pop. Remove from the heat and set aside.

Make the dressing: Toast the white sesame seeds in a skillet over medium heat until they start to pop. Combine the remaining dressing ingredients in a blender and blend for a few seconds. Add the white toasted sesame seeds and blend again for a few seconds to chop but not completely disintegrate the sesame seeds. Pour about 1 cup of the dressing onto the salad and toss well, adding more if you prefer (store the remaining dressing in a jar in the refrigerator up to 2 weeks for another use).

Refrigerate the salad until serving. It's best to let it sit for 30 minutes, if not longer. Sprinkle the black sesame seeds on top of the salad just before serving.

Grilled Chicken and Nectarine Salad
with Arugula, Almonds, and Fried Herb Cheese

Serves 4

In the deepest part of summer, you want a salad that is satisfying but also carries the brightest flavors of the season. Start with the best fresh nectarines you can find—the kind that are ripe but haven't yet become supersoft—and grill them, along with vegan chicken, for an arugula salad finished with almonds for crunch. Serve the salad as is or top it with Fried Herbed Cheese (recipe follows) if you're looking for something more decadent. Make the cheese while the grill heats.

GRILLED CHICKEN AND NECTARINES

¼ cup dry white wine

¼ cup extra-virgin olive oil, plus more for brushing the grill

Zest and juice of 1 large lemon

1 teaspoon Dijon mustard

1 clove garlic, grated

½ teaspoon kosher salt

¼ teaspoon freshly ground black pepper

10 ounces store-bought vegan chicken breasts, such as Gardein or Layonna, still frozen; or homemade Juicy Chicken (page 210) or Savory Roasted Chicken (page 212)

2 large ripe nectarines, each pitted and cut into 8 wedges

VINAIGRETTE

2 tablespoons sherry vinegar

1 teaspoon maple syrup

½ teaspoon Dijon mustard

Kosher salt and freshly ground black pepper

⅓ cup extra-virgin olive oil

First, marinate the chicken: In a large shallow bowl, whisk together the wine, olive oil, lemon zest and juice, mustard, garlic, salt, and pepper to blend. Add the chicken, turning to coat the pieces evenly, and let sit, covered, at room temperature for about 1 hour, turning occasionally, until the chicken is completely thawed.

Make the vinaigrette: In a small bowl, whisk together the vinegar, maple syrup, mustard, and salt and pepper to taste. While whisking, add the oil in a slow, steady stream, whisking until the oil is all blended in. Set aside. (The vinaigrette can be made a day ahead and refrigerated, covered, until ready to use.)

Heat a gas or charcoal grill to medium-high heat (about 400°F).

Brush the grill's cooking grates clean, then brush with oil. Remove the chicken from the marinade, letting any extra drip back into the bowl, and grill for 2 minutes per side (turning carefully), or until marked well on each side. Transfer the nectarine slices to the marinade, turn to coat, then add them to the grill as well, grilling for 2 to 3 minutes on each cut side, until well marked and beginning to soften. (You can also grill the chicken and nectarines on a stovetop grill pan over high heat.) Transfer the chicken and nectarines to a plate to rest.

RECIPE CONTINUES ▸▸

SALAD

4 ounces baby arugula
(about 4 packed cups)

½ cup toasted sliced almonds

2 whole large green onions (white
and green parts), thinly sliced

1½ cups Fried Herb Cheese
(optional; recipe follows)

Make the salad: In a bowl, toss the arugula, almonds, and green onions with vinaigrette to taste. Halve each chicken breast lengthwise, then cut the chicken crosswise into roughly ½-inch strips. Add the chicken and nectarines to the salad and toss gently to mix. Pile the salad onto four plates and serve immediately topped with Fried Herbed Cheese.

Fried Herbed Cheese

Makes about 1½ cups

My herbed cheese wheels have always been a hit on cheese platters, but the rounds also melt well and taste even better in that gooey half-melted stage. Which is why when you cut the wheels into little triangles, coat them in breadcrumbs, and sauté them in butter till they crisp, they become the perfect topping for a simple green salad or my Grilled Chicken and Nectarine Salad with Arugula, Almonds, and Fried Herb Cheese (page 31). These artisanal cheese wheels are pricey, however, so if you'd prefer to make something yourself, give the Homemade Paneer a spin.

About 6.5 ounces store-bought artisan vegan cheese wheel, such as Miyoko's Double Cream Classic Chive or Double Cream Garlic Herb, or Treeline, any flavor; or Homemade Paneer (page 233)

¼ cup vegan scrambled egg batter, such as Just Egg or Follow Your Heart, or ¼ cup water plus 2 teaspoons ground flaxseed to make a flax egg

½ cup Italian-style breadcrumbs

2 tablespoons vegan butter, such as Miyoko's

Cut the cheese wheel into eight equal wedges. If you are making a flax egg, combine the water and ground flaxseed in a bowl, whisk, and let sit for 2 to 3 minutes to thicken slightly. Put the egg and breadcrumbs into separate small bowls. Working with one wedge at a time, dip the cheese first into the egg, turning gently to coat it on all sides, then into the breadcrumbs, making sure the egg is completely covered on all sides. Set the prepared cheese aside.

Heat a small nonstick skillet over medium heat. Add 1 tablespoon of the butter. When totally melted, add the cheese wedges and cook for about 1 minute per side, until browned and crisp, about 5 minutes total, adding a bit of the remaining 1 tablespoon butter to the pan at each turn to make sure the pan doesn't go dry. When all sides of the cheese are browned—make sure you get the small edge side—gently transfer them to a plate and set aside. (They'll be quite soft.) Serve warm.

Buffalo NotCobb Salad

Serves 4

If you're tasked with trying to prove how great eating animal-free can be, here is a show-off salad that is at home for a ladies' luncheon or a big family reunion.

DRESSING

½ cup vegan mayonnaise

¼ cup extra-virgin olive oil

3 tablespoons apple cider vinegar

2 tablespoons nutritional yeast (see Glossary)

2 tablespoons vegan sour cream, such as Kite Hill, Ripple, or Forager

1 tablespoon chopped fresh dill

4 green onions (light green and white parts only), very finely chopped

1 clove garlic, grated

Kosher salt and freshly ground black pepper

SALAD

4 tablespoons vegan butter, such as Miyoko's, melted

¼ cup vegan chicken wing hot sauce, such as Frank's RedHot

8 ounces silken tofu

¼ teaspoon black salt (kala namak; see Glossary)

8 ounces store-bought vegan bacon, such as Lightlife, Sweet Earth, or Uptons; or homemade King Trumpet Mushroom Bacon (page 205)

1 (12-ounce) head romaine lettuce

10 ounces store-bought vegan chicken breasts, such as Gardein or Layonna, cooked according to package instructions; or homemade Juicy Chicken (page 210) or Savory Roasted Chicken (page 212)

2 ripe avocados, sliced

1 pint cherry tomatoes, halved

Make the dressing: In a small bowl, whisk together the mayonnaise, olive oil, vinegar, nutritional yeast, sour cream, dill, green onions, and garlic until you have a thick, smooth dressing. Season with salt and pepper and set aside.

Make the salad: In a medium bowl, stir together the melted butter and hot sauce. Set this buffalo sauce aside to cool slightly.

In a small nonstick skillet, mash the tofu over medium heat into bite-size pieces. Cook for about 2 minutes, cooking and stirring, then pour off any liquid and transfer the tofu to a paper towel–lined plate. The idea here is to rid the tofu of water and firm up the tofu so it resembles egg whites in texture—it doesn't need to brown. Sprinkle the tofu with black salt and stir gently. Cook the bacon according to package instructions, then chop.

Cut the lettuce and chicken into bite-size pieces. Arrange the lettuce, avocados, tomatoes, and bacon on a large platter. Just before serving, fold the chicken into the buffalo sauce and add it to the platter. Top the salad with the tofu and serve immediately, with the dressing alongside or drizzled over everything.

Blasted Brussels Sprouts with Balsamic and Bacon

Serves 4 to 6

Saying these sweet, crisp Brussels sprouts require two forms of cooking is sort of misleading. It's true, but for the effort you also get the best of both cooking methods: Steaming cooks the sprouts all the way through, so they achieve a soft, creamy center, and then blasting them with high heat in the oven makes their outsides brown until they're just short of burnt and packed with flavor. Paired with crunchy, chewy bacon bits that caramelize on the pan in balsamic vinegar, it's a bull's-eye side dish for Pork Tenderlove (page 199) or Hasselback Steak with Balsamic Chimichurri Sauce (page 124), but I'm the type to eat the entire plate by myself for lunch. If you're making the King Trumpet Mushroom Bacon, be sure to get it good and crisp for this!

1 pound medium Brussels sprouts, ends trimmed, left whole

¾ cup chopped homemade King Trumpet Mushroom Bacon (preferred; page 205), or 3 ounces store-bought vegan bacon, such as Lightlife or Sweet Earth, cut into ¼-inch pieces

2 tablespoons extra-virgin olive oil

Kosher salt and freshly ground black pepper

2 tablespoons balsamic vinegar

Flaky sea salt for serving

Set an oven rack to the middle position and preheat the oven to 500°F.

Prepare a medium to large pot for steaming: Fill the pot with about an inch of water and set a steaming basket inside. (The water shouldn't come up above the level of the steamer.) Bring to a boil over high heat, then add the Brussels sprouts, cover, reduce the heat to low, and steam for 10 minutes. Transfer the sprouts to a sheet pan and let cool for about 5 minutes, until the outer leaves begin to look dry.

If using homemade bacon, with your hands, toss the sprouts in the oil until they're well coated on all sides, then season generously with kosher salt and pepper. If you're using store-bought bacon, combine the oil and bacon in a small skillet over medium-high heat. Cook for about 3 minutes, stirring frequently, until the bacon begins to crisp. Drain the bacon through a sieve held over the cooling sprouts, so the bacon-scented oil coats them all, then set the bacon aside. Continue as for homemade bacon.

Roast the oiled sprouts for 10 minutes, then add the reserved bacon and drizzle the vinegar all over the pan. Shake the pan to rotate the sprouts and distribute the vinegar, then roast for 3 more minutes, or until the bacon is crisp and the sprouts are deeply browned and totally soft in the centers. Pile the sprouts onto a serving platter, top with all the bacon, shower with flaky sea salt, and serve immediately.

Butter-Braised Endive with Bacon Gremolata

Serves 4 to 6

Only the French could get away with braising leaves in butter and passing them off as a virtuous side dish. But they do, and so will I: If you simmer endive slowly in vegan butter, it takes on a creamy, silky quality quite different from the raw version of itself. It's less bitter, more comforting. Serve it alongside Boeuf Bourguignon (page 110), Coq au Vin (page 122), or Brisket Roulade with Duxelles and Truffle Demi-Glace (page 139).

Gremolata is typically a mixture of parsley, lemon, and garlic that's sprinkled conservatively over meat dishes—but here, with the bacon at center stage, it's a more liberal sprinkling. You can also try the gremolata itself sprinkled on baked potatoes, steamed green beans, or avocado toast.

6 Belgian endives (about 1 pound), halved lengthwise

Kosher salt and freshly ground black pepper

6 tablespoons vegan butter, such as Miyoko's, cut into tablespoon-size chunks

2 tablespoons extra-virgin olive oil

½ cup finely chopped homemade King Trumpet Mushroom Bacon (preferred; page 205) or store-bought vegan bacon, such as Lightlife or Sweet Earth

1 large clove garlic, grated

½ cup finely chopped fresh Italian parsley

1 teaspoon zest and squeeze of juice from 1 navel orange

1 teaspoon zest and squeeze of juice from 1 medium lemon

Season the endive with salt and pepper on the cut sides.

In a nonstick pan large enough to hold all the endive cut sides down (a 12-inch pan works well), melt 4 tablespoons of the butter over medium heat. When the butter foams, add all of the endive in a sunburst pattern, cut sides down. Top with the remaining 2 butter chunks, cover, and cook for 10 minutes. Remove the lid, increase the heat to high, and cook for another 3 minutes, or until the cut sides have browned. Gently transfer the endive to a serving platter, browned sides up, allowing any extra butter to drip back into the pan first.

While the endive braises, make the gremolata: Heat a small nonstick skillet over medium-high heat. If you're using homemade bacon, add the bacon and garlic and cook, stirring for 1 minute, to warm and take the edge off the garlic; if you're using store-bought bacon, cook the bacon alone for about 3 minutes, stirring frequently, until the bacon begins to crisp. Add the garlic and cook for 1 minute. For both versions, now transfer the mixture to a paper towel–lined bowl, then a small bowl, and stir together the bacon mixture, parsley, and zests from the orange and lemon. Season with salt and pepper.

When the endive is ready, sprinkle the gremolata over the endive and serve immediately, topped with hearty squeezes of orange juice and lemon juice around the platter.

Grilled Mexican Street Corn

Serves 4

For the uninitiated, Mexican street corn, or elote, can be mind-blowing. Rather than lather corn with plain old butter and maybe a sprinkling of salt, many street vendors south of the border smear it with mayonnaise, then shower it with a mix of cotija (a crumbly Mexican cheese), chile powder, chopped cilantro, and sometimes a squeeze of lime. At home, it's a great way to move a simple side dish to center stage. My vegan take is similar, relying on vegan feta, a dash of cumin for extra earthiness, and a bit of what I called Chorizo Dust for heat and meaty flavor. The salad version is great with the tamales on page 133.

You can also turn this into a delicious warm salad; just cut the grilled corn off the cob, transfer it to a small serving bowl, and mix it with the spiced mayonnaise mixture. Double the feta and cilantro and fold it into the salad right at the end with the chorizo.

4 ears corn (white or yellow), shucked

1 to 2 tablespoons extra-virgin olive oil for brushing the corn

Kosher salt and freshly ground black pepper

¼ cup vegan mayonnaise

½ teaspoon chile powder, such as chipotle or ancho chile

½ teaspoon ground cumin

¼ cup finely chopped vegan feta cheese

1 tablespoon finely chopped fresh cilantro

2 tablespoons Chorizo Dust (recipe follows)

4 lime wedges

Heat a gas or charcoal grill over medium-high heat (about 400°F). Brush the corn on all sides with olive oil, then season lightly all over with salt and pepper. Brush the cooking grates clean, then grill the corn for 8 to 10 minutes, turning every few minutes, until the kernels are cooked through all over and browned in spots. (You can also grill the corn on a stovetop grill pan over high heat.)

While the corn cooks, in a small bowl, stir together the mayonnaise, chile powder, cumin, and 1 teaspoon salt. Using the back of a spoon, smear each hot corn cob with a scant tablespoon of the spiced mayonnaise mixture. (It's okay if you wind up using your hands.) Arrange the corn on a platter, sprinkle with the cheese, cilantro, and Chorizo Dust, and top with a grinding of pepper. Serve immediately with lime wedges. Cut any leftover corn off the cob and refrigerate to use for salads, burritos, or rice bowls.

RECIPE CONTINUES ➤➤

Chorizo Dust

Makes ½ cup

2 tablespoons extra-virgin olive oil

If you cook the oil out of soy chorizo, it makes delicious little crumbles—like a Mexican-inspired version of bacon bits. In addition to the street corn on the previous page, you can sprinkle it into an avocado half at snack time or use it as a topping for scrambled eggs.

6 ounces vegan chorizo,
such as Soyrizo or Upton's

Heat a nonstick skillet over medium heat. Add the oil, then the chorizo, and cook, stirring and breaking up the meat occasionally, for 10 minutes, or until the chorizo is very well cooked and beginning to fall apart. Reduce the heat to the lowest setting and cook for another 10 minutes, stirring and continuing to break it up, until the chorizo appears dry. Transfer the chorizo to a paper towel–lined plate to drain, then transfer it to a new paper towel. Fold the paper towel's edges over the meat and rub it gently to encourage the meat to break into even smaller pieces. Use immediately, or refrigerate, covered, for up to 3 days. To revive, microwave for about 30 seconds before using.

Kale and Sausage Gratin

Serves 4 to 6

A good long stint in the oven gives this hearty kale gratin a few hard edges on the outside, but once you dig in, you'll find sweetness and depth—and it's the combination of the various textures that makes it work. Know that when you pile the kale into a towering mass in the baking dish, it's easy to believe it just might not fit. Trust the oven to talk down the kale while you do something else, like preparing an accompaniment, such as the Sunday Night Meatloaf (page 54) or Rotisserie Chicken (page 52).

1 lightly packed cup (about 1.5 ounces) finely grated store-bought vegan Parmesan, such as Violife or Follow Your Heart, or a half-and-half mixture of grated Parmesan and grated smoked mozzarella, such as Miyoko's

¾ cup unsweetened plain or "original" flavor oat milk

1 (5.4-ounce) can unsweetened coconut cream

¼ cup plain vegan cream cheese, such as Miyoko's or Kite Hill

2 teaspoons cornstarch

½ teaspoon kosher salt

¼ teaspoon freshly ground black pepper

Dash of freshly grated nutmeg

1¼ pounds kale (about 3 bunches, and any mix of red, green, or lacinato kale will do), stems removed, chopped into 2-inch pieces

2 vegan Italian sausages (about 7 ounces), such as Beyond Meat, Field Roast, or Tofurky, halved lengthwise, then cut into ¼-inch half-moons (precooking according to package instructions will be required for Beyond Meat or other "raw" type sausages)

2 tablespoons pine nuts, toasted (see Note)

Preheat the oven to 375°F. Place an 11-inch oval baking dish (or similar) on a sheet pan and set aside.

In a large bowl, whisk together the Parmesan cheese, oat milk, coconut cream, cream cheese, cornstarch, salt, pepper, and nutmeg until evenly distributed; you'll have to work at the coconut cream a little. Add the kale and fold it in until the cream mixture coats all the leaves. (Hands work best here!) Fold in the sausage, then transfer the mixture to the baking dish, patting the kale in to make it all somehow fit. Bake for 45 minutes, or until the liquid is simmering and the kale on top is well browned and crisp. Top with the pine nuts and serve warm or at room temperature.

Note: If you can't find toasted pine nuts, toss raw pine nuts in a skillet over low heat for 2 to 3 minutes, until nutty brown.

Roasted Cauliflower Steaks with Hot Chorizo Vinaigrette

Serves 4

Cauliflower steak is all the rage and seems to be loved by both vegans and omnivores. Roasting caramelizes the sweetness of the cauliflower and concentrates the flavor, and when it's gussied up with a tangy chorizo vinaigrette, the rich, spicy bits of soy chorizo get lodged between its branches, making every bite a little flavor explosion. Serve it as a side dish for Charbroiled Succulent Steak (page 188) or even mac and cheese, or make it the main event, piled onto quinoa or rice with a side of beans (and maybe some salsa and a sliced avocado) for an instant rice bowl.

1 (2½-pound) head cauliflower

9 tablespoons extra-virgin olive oil

Kosher salt and freshly ground black pepper

3 ounces vegan chorizo, such as Soyrizo or Upton's

1 clove garlic, grated

3 tablespoons apple cider vinegar

2 tablespoons finely chopped fresh parsley

Preheat the oven to 400°F. Line a sheet pan with parchment paper and set aside.

Break away all the thick stems and leaves from the bottom of the cauliflower. Trim the thick stalk down to just below the bottom of the cauliflower head, then place the head cut side down on a cutting board and slice it into 1-inch-thick slabs. Transfer the cauliflower steaks to the prepared sheet pan. (It's okay if some of them fall apart.) Brush the cauliflower generously with 3 tablespoons of the olive oil and season with salt and pepper on both sides. Roast for 25 to 30 minutes, flipping the cauliflower about halfway through, until both sides are browned and the cauliflower is tender.

After you flip the cauliflower, in a large nonstick pan, heat 3 tablespoons of the olive oil over medium-high heat. When the oil shimmers, add the chorizo and garlic and cook, stirring frequently, until the chorizo is browned, crumbly, and cooked through, about 3 minutes. Add the vinegar and season with salt and pepper, then turn the heat off and let sit until the cauliflower is cooked.

Transfer the roasted cauliflower to a platter. Bring the chorizo mixture back to a simmer just to reheat it, stir in the remaining 3 tablespoons olive oil, then pour the chorizo mixture all over the cauliflower. Shower with the parsley and serve immediately.

CHAPTER 2

Comfort the Soul

Comfort food can mean different things to different people. For me, because I grew up partly in Japan, at the end of a rough day I crave a bowl of rice with miso soup. For others, it's BBQ ribs, or mac and cheese, or fried chicken, and yet for others, it's a shepherd's pie. Whatever form it comes in, whatever country you're from, we all know that some foods were designed to ease the pain of a difficult day, to help us unwind, to feed our soul. They may not be the fanciest or the most complex; in fact, most are simple without layers and layers of flavor, but they are honest. And true. And they work every time.

In this chapter, you'll find a variety of foods that soothe and nourish the spirit. Yes, there's the finger-lickin' good Colonel Compassion's Best-Ever Buttermilk Fried Chicken (page 46), because how could you have a chapter on comfort foods without this? But not every recipe is necessarily all-American—some are from far-flung corners of the world but still provide that hearty satisfaction required of comfort foods. From the Japanese pork cutlet Tonkatsu (page 70), to an Italian-rooted calzone (page 63) and enchiladas with a twist (page 76), all of these dishes will take the stress out of your day and put a smile on your face.

Colonel Compassion's Best-Ever Buttermilk Fried Chicken

Serves 6 to 8 or more

Our hundred or so rescued chickens used to live in everything from battery cages to plastic boxes in classrooms. Some weren't so happy or healthy when they arrived at my animal sanctuary Rancho Compasión, but within days or weeks, they all learned to dust bathe, run around and peck at worms, and discover the joy of sunshine. It's hard for me to imagine that these curious, talkative creatures who sometimes jump in your lap and can recognize faces are considered "bird brained" and just something to be fried and eaten. With this tasty "fried chicken," you'll have a treat that you can even share with your favorite pet chicken (yes, they eat anything—just not potatoes). Crispy, crunchy, and full of flavor inside and outside, this better-than-the-Colonel's chicken is *bestest* made with Juicy Chicken or Savory Roasted Chicken, although you are welcome to use a commercial brand. Alternatively, I offer another approach made with frozen tofu where you can skip the seitan altogether and even make it gluten-free. But the secret is in the coating, which requires coating first in flour, dipping in batter, then re-coating in flour, resulting in the ultimate crispiness. Just make sure you make a lot, because it'll get eaten. As delicious as it is by itself, why not go all the way and accompany it with the rich gravy made from the frying oil and leftover batter? And as long as you're doing that, hey, don't forget the mashed potatoes and biscuits.

3 pounds Juicy Chicken (page 210) or Savory Roasted Chicken (page 212)

3 cups all-purpose or gluten-free flour

⅓ cup nutritional yeast (see Glossary)

4 teaspoons garlic powder

4 teaspoons onion powder

1 tablespoon poultry seasoning

1 teaspoon smoked paprika

1 teaspoon sea salt

1 teaspoon freshly ground black pepper

2 cups unsweetened plain or "original" flavor soy milk or oat milk, plus more if needed

Cut or tear the chicken into pieces according to the size you wish—bite-size for appetizers, bigger ones for meals. Combine the flour, nutritional yeast, garlic powder, onion powder, poultry seasoning, paprika, salt, and pepper in a large bowl and whisk well. Dip the pieces of chicken in the flour mixture to coat all sides and set aside. Divide the remaining flour mixture between the two bowls.

In a small bowl, combine the soy milk with the vinegar and allow it to sit for a couple of minutes, then mix in the mustard. Pour this into one of the bowls of the flour mixture and mix well with a fork to make a thick batter that will coat the chicken. If it is too thin, add a bit more flour from the other bowl; if it is too thick, add a bit more milk. Dip the pieces of chicken in the batter, then dip the battered chicken in the other bowl (with the other half of the flour mixture) to coat the batter with the flour mixture.

RECIPE CONTINUES ➳

2 tablespoons apple cider vinegar

3 tablespoons yellow mustard

About 2 cups neutral oil, such as sunflower, canola, avocado, or grapeseed

Meanwhile, heat at least ½ inch of oil in a deep frying pan that has a lid over high heat until the oil reaches about 350°F. If you don't have a thermometer, you can test the oil by dropping a little fingertip-size piece of chicken in the oil. It should hit the bottom, then immediately and steadily rise to the surface. Place the battered and floured chicken pieces in the oil, making sure not to overcrowd the pan—no more than three-quarters of the pan should have chicken in it. Cover the pan with the lid and cook until the chicken is a beautiful brown on the bottom, about 3 minutes, then flip the pieces to cook the other side. Drain on paper towels or brown paper bags. Repeat with the remaining pieces.

Variations

Chicken and Gravy: Use the leftover flour and batter to make gravy for your chicken. Here's how: After frying the chicken, pour out some of the oil so that there is only about ¼ inch left in the pan, leaving any bits and pieces of crispy batter or chicken in the pan. Add the remaining flour, if any, or some of the batter. Since it's hard to say how much will be left, don't add it all at once, only enough so that when you stir it with the remaining oil it forms a loose roux. Cook it for a couple of minutes, then add hot water—maybe 3 to 4 cups—whisking all the while, until thickened. Season with salt and pepper and a dash or two of soy sauce. The cooking oil itself will add a lot of flavor—you might be surprised if you haven't made gravy this way before, so you needn't add more in terms of seasonings. Enjoy the gravy poured over the fried chicken, along with mashed potatoes and biscuits if you've given in to total indulgence.

Frozen Tofu Version (can be gluten-free): Freeze 2 pounds of medium or firm tofu for at least 1 week (you can freeze it right in the tub). The tofu will get firmer the longer it freezes, so you can have it in the freezer for months if you like. When you are ready to use it, thaw it—you can do so on your counter overnight or in a bowl of hot water. After the tofu has thawed, squeeze the water out of it. You'll find that it is now like a dry sponge. In a bowl, combine 3 cups vegan chicken broth (you can use water and a vegan chicken bouillon); ¼ cup nutritional yeast (see Glossary); 2 tablespoons soy sauce, tamari, or Bragg Liquid Aminos; and 2 teaspoons poultry seasoning. Tear the tofu into big chunks and marinate in the mixture for at least 1 hour, until it has absorbed the marinade. Now proceed to coat the tofu in the all-purpose or gluten-free flour and batter and fry as directed in the main recipe.

Meaty, Smoky Chili

Serves 4 to 6

I do a ton of traveling. Whether it's Italy or Vietnam or Singapore, chances are that in a given month, I'm darting off to some far-flung location, mostly for business but often for fun. Sometimes the most pleasure comes when I walk in the door—and back to my own kitchen. Here's a spicy homecoming chili, just right as the hearty, comforting meal you need after days on the road. With a little advance planning, it's the kind of thing you can shop for before you leave. Another bonus: After about fifteen minutes of attention, it sits on the stove happily on its own, while you attend to higher-priority things, like convincing your pets you do indeed still love them. Note that this is one of the times you don't want to drain canned beans; the thick liquid from the can helps thicken the chili.

Tip: Different vegan meats break down at different rates when simmered for a long time, which is why it's best to add in the meat toward the end. Cook the beef according to the instructions on the package: Some call for additional oil, but some don't. The instructions below are for Beyond Meat's Beyond Beef.

2 tablespoons extra-virgin olive oil

1 yellow or white onion, finely chopped

4 cloves garlic, finely chopped

1 tablespoon chipotle chile powder

1½ teaspoons ground cumin

1 teaspoon dried oregano

½ teaspoon ground coriander

1 (15-ounce) can tomato sauce

1 (28-ounce) can diced tomatoes

1 (15-ounce) can low-sodium black beans, not drained

In a large soup pot, heat the olive oil over medium heat. Add the onions and cook, stirring occasionally, for 4 minutes, or until they begin to soften. Add the garlic and cook for another minute or so, stirring frequently. Stir in the chile powder, cumin, oregano, and coriander until well blended, then stir a moment or so more to toast the spices, until the mixture is super fragrant. Add the tomato sauce, stirring well to scrape any browned bits off the bottom of the pot, then add the diced tomatoes, black beans, pinto beans, kidney beans, agave, the chipotle chile, soy sauce, and umami powder, stir to blend, and bring to a simmer. Reduce the heat to the lowest setting and cook for about 1 hour, stirring whenever you happen to walk by, until thicker and sticking to the pan at the edges. (You can add water as needed to make a thinner chili, if you prefer.)

RECIPE CONTINUES ▶▸

1 (15-ounce) can low-sodium pinto beans, not drained

1 (15-ounce) can low-sodium kidney beans, not drained

2 tablespoons agave nectar, sugar, or maple syrup

2 tablespoons chopped chipotle chile in adobo (or to taste)

1½ tablespoons soy sauce, tamari, or Bragg Liquid Aminos (see Glossary)

1 tablespoon umami powder or red miso

1 pound store-bought "raw" type vegan ground beef, such as Beyond Meat, Hungry Planet, Lightlife, Meatless Farm, Abbot's Butcher, or Sweet Earth; or Homemade "Raw" Ground Beef (page 193)

Kosher salt and freshly ground black pepper

Vegan sour cream, such as Kite Hill or Forager, for serving

Shredded vegan cheddar cheese, such as Miyoko's or Violife, for serving

Heat a large nonstick skillet over medium-high heat. Add the beef in pieces so they cover all of the pan and cook for 2 to 3 minutes, until well browned, then turn the beef and cook for another 3 to 4 minutes, breaking it up into small pieces with a sturdy spatula, until the beef is crumbly and uniformly browned. Set aside.

After the chili has simmered for about 55 minutes, stir in the cooked beef and cook for another 5 minutes or so to blend the flavors. Season with salt and pepper. Serve the chili piping hot, topped with a dollop of sour cream and a good shower of cheese. You can also let the chili cool to room temperature and refrigerate, covered, for up to 3 days before reheating and serving. Or make this before you go on a trip and freeze, where it will keep for 2 to 3 months. Then when you return, you can have an almost instant meal to welcome you home in comfort.

Meet the Animals

Louie, our feisty 1,400-pound Black Angus steer, might have ended up as a bowl of chili or a steak. He was off to the county fair, where he would have been auctioned off and gone home to someone's freezer in neatly wrapped packets. Louie was raised by a teenage girl as part of the FFA (Future Farmers of America), a school program in which kids raise farm animals then auction them off at the county fair. This young lady fell in love with Louie's penchant for play and his strong-headed but sweet personality and found herself unable to see him sold for slaughter. Her family forced her to take him to the county fair anyway, where she got to thinking fast: A shot of dewormer would disqualify him for slaughter. She and Louie were kicked out of the fair, after which she happily brought him to Rancho Compasión, where he will live out his life with his dairy cow girlfriend, Angel.

Rotisserie Chicken

Serves 6 to 8

I do recall how as a child I loved going to the grocery store with my father and bringing home a rotisserie chicken on special occasions. Of course, the only chickens I bring home now are fully alive, rescued from the fate of slaughter, who get to spend the rest of their days dust-bathing and pecking at worms and grass at Rancho Compasión. No, this doesn't taste exactly as I remember it from over fifty years ago, but it's pretty darn tasty. Even a sub par whole vegan chicken I bought at a Chinese grocer fared well with this treatment. The first step is to brine the featherless "bird" for a good day, infusing it with freshness and ramping up the juiciness. Then it's rubbed with a basting butter and wrapped in yuba, which turns into a succulent skin. Serve it with some good old potato salad or mashed potatoes and a big green salad and have yourself a traditional American dinner.

Meet the Animals

Did you know that chickens make more than thirty different sounds, each with a different meaning? From the gentle cooing of happy hens to high-pitched cries warning of a predator to the bold and loud announcements that they've laid an egg to the rhythmic staccato of a rooster inviting his hens to a pile of worms, chickens are highly vocal, communicative, and intelligent creatures. Having rescued hundreds of chickens, I've come to recognize that they are similar to people in many ways: Some are highly social with humans, wanting to connect and sit in your lap, while others want nothing to do with you; some have a best friend or two, while others are loners; some are fearless, while others are meek. Just like humans, chickens come in all shapes and sizes in body and personality. Birds of a flock—they say. When you look beyond the flock, what you see are individuals.

4 cups water

1 lemon, sliced

8 cloves garlic, peeled and smashed

1 tablespoon black peppercorns

1 tablespoon sugar

1 tablespoon kosher salt

½ cup chopped fresh parsley

6 sprigs fresh thyme

3 sprigs fresh rosemary

CHICKEN

1 whole homemade Juicy Chicken (about 2 pounds, page 210) or Savory Roasted Chicken (page 212); or store-bought chicken (check Asian grocery stores for whole vegan chickens)

1 large sheet frozen yuba (see Glossary)

BASTING BUTTER

½ cup vegan butter, such as Miyoko's, melted

2 teaspoons smoked paprika

1 teaspoon dried rubbed sage

1 teaspoon dried thyme

1 teaspoon garlic powder

1 teaspoon onion powder

½ teaspoon sea salt

¼ teaspoon freshly ground black pepper

Make the brine: Make the brine 24 hours in advance of baking, as you'll want to brine your chicken a good long time for the most flavor. Combine all of the ingredients for the brine in a large bowl and mix well. Take your chicken—whichever one you choose—and put it in the brine. The brine should cover it. Cover the bowl and put it in the refrigerator for at least 24 hours or up to 48.

When you are ready to bake, preheat the oven to 375°F.

Make the basting butter: Combine the melted butter with the smoked paprika, sage, thyme, garlic powder, onion powder, sea salt, and pepper.

Run the piece of yuba under cold water for a few seconds. Set it aside for a minute to become pliable, then squeeze it gently to remove excess water. Take the chicken and rub some of the basting butter over the entire surface. As best as you can, take the yuba and wrap the chicken with it, smoothing out the lumps and wrinkles so that it can resemble "skin." Place it in a baking dish, then baste the entire yuba-wrapped chicken with the remaining basting butter. Bake for about 40 minutes, until beautifully browned, pulling the chicken out of the oven about halfway through to baste with the butter in the dish. Baste again after pulling it out of the oven in order to soften the skin slightly, as baking will render it crispy.

Sunday Night Meatloaf

Serves 6 to 8

You don't need gravy with this flavorful meatloaf made from a combination of vegan ground beef and sausages with a good dose of mushroom duxelles, herbs, and spices. The glaze is not the usual sweet ketchupy concoction but a bit more complex and savory, with the base of juice extracted from the mushrooms and a hint of smoked paprika. It might help you remember your mother's meatloaf, but you'll probably think it's better.

MEATLOAF

1 pound store-bought "raw" type vegan ground beef, such as Beyond Meat, Hungry Planet, Meatless Farm, or Lightlife

2 (7-ounce) "raw" type vegan sausages, such as Beyond Meat or Lightlife

½ yellow or white onion, roughly diced (about ⅔ cup)

6 cloves garlic, peeled

8 ounces white or cremini mushrooms, cut in quarters

1 tablespoon olive oil

Dash of sea salt

½ cup finely diced red bell pepper

½ cup finely diced carrot

¼ cup tomato paste

3 tablespoons Bragg Liquid Aminos (see Glossary)

Make the meatloaf: Preheat the oven to 350°F. Grease a baking dish that is approximately 9 by 13 inches.

In a large bowl, combine the vegan ground beef and sausages, breaking up the sausages with your hands.

In a food processor, pulse the onion and garlic until very finely minced. Add them to the bowl.

Without washing the food processor, process the mushrooms until they are very finely minced, but don't overprocess and let them turn into a puree. Remove the mushrooms and place them in the middle of a piece of cheesecloth or a tea towel. Gather up the fabric and squeeze the mushrooms over a small bowl to extract their juice and collect it in the bowl. Reserve this juice for the glaze.

In a skillet, heat the oil over medium heat, then add the mushrooms and salt. Cook the mushrooms until they turn from pink to brown and look dry, just a minute or two. Add them to the bowl, along with the bell pepper and carrot. Add the tomato paste, liquid aminos, miso, nutritional yeast, smoked paprika, basil, marjoram, oregano, rosemary, allspice, and black pepper and mix well with a wooden spoon or with your hands.

2 tablespoons chickpea miso
or white soy miso

2 tablespoons nutritional yeast
(see Glossary)

1 tablespoon smoked paprika

1 tablespoon dried basil

1 teaspoon dried marjoram

1 teaspoon dried oregano

1 teaspoon dried rosemary

1½ teaspoons ground allspice

½ teaspoon freshly ground
black pepper

GLAZE

2 to 3 tablespoons juice from
mushrooms (see above)

2 tablespoons tomato paste

2 tablespoons soy sauce

1 tablespoon cornstarch or arrowroot

1 tablespoon maple syrup

½ teaspoon smoked paprika

In the prepared baking dish, form a loaf with the mixture. With your fingers, make a ½-inch indentation down the middle running the entire length (this cavity will capture some of the glaze so it doesn't all run off).

Make the glaze and bake: In a bowl, whisk the mushroom juice, tomato paste, soy sauce, cornstarch, maple syrup, and smoked paprika until smooth. Cover the loaf with this mixture using a rubber spatula. Bake for about 1¼ hours, until the top middle feels springy and firm. Let cool for 15 minutes before cutting.

The Burger Trilogy

Let's just say it: No matter what vegan meat technology comes our way, there will always be those who scoff at the mere idea of a vegan burger. It's the harbinger of vegan meat-making success, but it's also the industry's whipping boy. Article after article chronicles side-by-side taste comparisons of burgers made with beef, Beyond Meat, and the Impossible Burger (not to mention the rest of the competitors). Inevitably, photos show naked burgers on anemic buns, vying for attention—but too often, the point of a burger is totally forgotten. Of course, no one will switch from beef to Beyond if their regular burger comes loaded with kimchi and a fried egg while the Beyond comes plain. We just need to admit it: Half the fun is in the toppings.

I'd challenge any hard-core meat eater to remember their last plain burger. (It's not as good, right?) Then I'd challenge them to taste one of these—a trilogy of well-garnished burgers, all dressed with toppings that can be made in about the time it takes to cook the burger itself. Choose your own adventure, or make up your own. Any way you slice it, it will be delicious—for you and for the person who sees a vegan burger as a worst-case scenario. (Just you wait.) For extra deliciousness, smear the buns with vegan butter and toast them cut side down in a skillet over medium heat for 2 minutes or so while the burgers cook.

RECIPE CONTINUES ▶▶

Greek Burger with Feta and Quick Kalamata Tapenade

Makes 4 burgers

4 store-bought vegan burgers, any type, such as Beyond, Gardein, Field Roast, or Hungry Planet; or homemade, such as Chicken Burgers (page 219) or burgers from Instant Burger, Patty, Meatball, and Crumbles Mix (page 196)

Kosher salt and freshly ground black pepper

1 cup pitted kalamata olives

2 tablespoons drained capers

2 tablespoons roughly chopped fresh parsley

1 tablespoon extra-virgin olive oil

4 vegan burger buns

4 leaves Bibb or green leaf lettuce, torn if large

4 ounces vegan feta cheese, such as Violife, cut into ½-inch cubes

2-inch section English cucumber, halved lengthwise and thinly sliced crosswise

Heat a large nonstick skillet over medium-high heat. Add the burgers, season with salt and pepper, and cook for about 6 minutes, turning halfway through, until well browned on both sides. (Use the instructions on your burgers' packaging instead, if it's different.)

Meanwhile, in a food processor, blitz together the olives, capers, parsley, olive oil, and a good grind of pepper until you get a chunky tapenade, about 10 pulses.

Transfer the burgers to the bun bottoms, then top with the lettuce, tapenade to taste, cheese, and cucumber slices. Add the top bun and serve immediately.

Smoky Truffled Mushroom Burger

Makes 4 burgers

2 tablespoons extra-virgin olive oil

1 large shallot, halved and thinly sliced

1 pound cremini mushrooms, sliced

Kosher salt and freshly ground black pepper

2 tablespoons dry white wine

1 teaspoon chopped fresh thyme

2 tablespoons vegan butter, such as Miyoko's

1 tablespoon finely chopped fresh parsley

4 store-bought vegan burgers, any type, such as Beyond, Gardein, Field Roast, or Hungry Planet; or homemade, such as Chicken Burgers (page 219) or burgers from Instant Burger, Patty, Meatball, and Crumbles Mix (page 196)

4 ounces vegan smoked mozzarella or other vegan smoked cheese, such as Miyoko's or Violife, thinly sliced

4 vegan burger buns

Truffle oil for serving (see Note, opposite)

In a large skillet, heat the olive oil over medium heat. Add the shallots and cook, stirring, for 3 minutes, or until they begin to soften. Add the mushrooms, season with salt and pepper, and cook, stirring occasionally, until the mushrooms have lost all their moisture and are well browned, about 10 minutes. Add the wine and the thyme and cook, stirring for 2 minutes more, or until the wine has evaporated. Add the butter and parsley, stir until the butter is absorbed, then set the pan aside.

Note: Not all truffle oil is created equal. Taste yours and decide how much to add based on how strong it is and how much truffle flavor is right for your burger.

Meanwhile, heat a large nonstick skillet over medium-high heat. Add the burgers, season with salt and pepper, and cook for about 6 minutes, turning halfway through, until well browned on both sides. (Use the instructions on your burgers' packaging instead, if it's different.) Place the cheese slices on the burgers, turn off the heat, cover the pan, and set aside for the cheese to warm through, about 2 minutes. Transfer the burgers to the bun bottoms, then divide the mushroom mixture over the burgers evenly, drizzle with truffle oil (see Note), add the top buns, and serve immediately.

Kimchi Burger with Korean Special Sauce

Makes 4 burgers

4 store-bought vegan burgers, any type, such as Beyond, Meatless Farm, Field Roast, or Hungry Planet; or homemade, such as Chicken Burgers (page 219), or burgers from Instant Burger, Patty, Meatball, and Crumbles Mix (page 196)

Kosher salt and freshly ground black pepper

2 teaspoons doenjang (Korean soybean paste) or red miso paste

2 teaspoons gochujang (Korean chile paste)

¾ teaspoon sugar

2 teaspoons water

¼ cup vegan mayonnaise

1 cup vegan kimchi, chopped if pieces are large

¾ cup bean sprouts

4 small radishes, thinly sliced

¼ cup chopped fresh cilantro

4 vegan burger buns

Heat a large nonstick skillet over medium-high heat. Add the burgers, season with salt and pepper, and cook for about 6 minutes, turning halfway through, until well browned on both sides. (Use the instructions on your burgers' packaging instead, if it's different.)

Meanwhile, in a small bowl, mash together the doenjang, gochujang, sugar, and water to blend, then add the mayonnaise and stir until smooth. Add the kimchi, bean sprouts, radishes, and cilantro and stir.

Transfer the burgers to the bun bottoms, then divide the kimchi mixture over the burgers, add the top buns, and serve immediately.

Jacob's New Orleans Authentic Jambalaya

Serves 6

I learned a couple of things when I visited New Orleans a few years ago. The first big thing was the correct pronunciation of "New Orleans." It's not *N'awlins*, no matter what some old blues tunes might have you thinking. And it's not *New Orleeeens*. It's just New *Orlins*. Plain and simple, the way the newscasters say it, not as we imagine that folks from there say it.

The other thing I learned was that I'd been making jambalaya wrong all these years by putting tomatoes in it. Turns out there are no tomatoes in authentic jambalaya—I learned this from a real live New "Orlins" chef, Jacob Seemann, who made me a giant portion of his vegan version that I could not stop eating. Jacob was gracious enough to share his recipe, which I share here with you.

6 tablespoons vegan butter, such as Miyoko's

1 cup diced yellow, white, or red onions

½ cup diced celery

½ cup diced green bell pepper

4 ounces sliced fresh shiitake mushrooms (2 cups)

1 tablespoon smoked paprika

4 large cloves garlic, chopped

1 cup large diced zucchini

1 cup large diced yellow squash

2 tablespoons Cajun seasoning, plus more to taste

2 cups long-grain white rice

½ cup chopped fresh parsley

4 cups vegetable broth, plus more if needed

½ cup chopped green onions (white and green parts)

In a large pot, melt 4 tablespoons of the butter over medium-high heat. Add the onions, celery, and bell pepper and sauté until translucent, about 5 minutes. Add the mushrooms and smoked paprika and continue to sauté for another 3 minutes or so until the vegetables are soft. Add the garlic, zucchini, yellow squash, and Cajun seasoning and cook for another 3 minutes or so until the squash is soft.

Add the rice and parsley and turn up the heat to high. Continue cooking, stirring, until you start to see browning and caramelization on the bottom of the pan and everything starts to stick to the bottom, about 5 minutes— this is what gives jambalaya its distinct flavor. Don't worry about a bit of sticking, as it will all lift off once the broth is added.

Add 1 cup of the vegetable broth to deglaze the pan and get the rice to soak up all the delicious caramelized flavor, then throw in the green onions and liquid aminos. Cook for a minute, add the remaining 3 cups broth, the sausage, and chicken, and give it a stir, then bring it to a boil. At this point, taste a bit of the broth and decide whether or not to add up to 2 tablespoons more Cajun seasoning, as different brands vary greatly in intensity of heat and level of salt. Cover the pot, reduce the heat to a low simmer, and cook for about 20 minutes. As it cooks, give the pot a stir

2 tablespoons Bragg Liquid Aminos
(see Glossary)

2 vegan Field Roast Smoked Apple Sage
Sausages or Hot Italian Beyond Sausages

1 cup store-bought vegan chicken strips
or chunks, such as The Better Chew,
Plant Ranch, No Evil Foods, Gardein,
or Tofurky; or homemade Juicy Chicken
(page 210) or Savory Roasted Chicken
(page 212)

once or twice. If, during cooking, the rice is still hard and it looks like you are running out of liquid in the pot, add an additional ½ cup broth. When the broth is completely absorbed, remove from heat, stir, and if desired, stir in the remaining 2 tablespoons vegan butter to enrich the dish (see Note). Let the dish sit, covered, for 5 minutes before serving.

Note: You can skip the additional butter enrichment if you like, although it does add great flavor.

Sausage Calzones with Roasted Fennel and Preserved Lemon

Makes 4 large calzones

I'm obviously biased, but I'd give my mozzarella high marks in "works well with others." Here, it blankets a juicy, flavorful calzone filling with caramelized fennel, sausages with a bit of a bite, and spunky strips of preserved lemon. Note that we're not talking about a Jersey-style calzone here—it's still large, but lighter inside than the choices you made late at night in college, with a sauce made simply from roasted cherry tomatoes and olive oil.

Also, remember that purchasing premade pizza dough is not a sin. If it makes your life easier, do that—just make sure you let the dough come to room temperature before you roll it out. You'll need about 2 pounds of dough to make 4 large calzones.

CRUST

1½ cups warm water

1 tablespoon instant yeast

3 to 3½ cups all-purpose flour, plus more for kneading the dough

1½ teaspoons kosher salt

1 tablespoon olive oil for oiling the bowl and sheet pan and brushing the calzones

FILLING

1 large fennel bulb (about 1 pound), cored and cut into 1-inch pieces

4 tablespoons extra-virgin olive oil

Kosher salt and freshly ground black pepper

1 pound cherry or grape tomatoes, halved

3 Italian-style "raw" type vegan sausages, such as Beyond Meat or Lightlife, cut into ¼-inch discs

2 cloves garlic, finely chopped

1 tablespoon chopped fresh rosemary

⅓ teaspoon red pepper flakes (optional)

Start the crust: In a measuring cup, whisk together the water and yeast and set aside for 5 minutes to allow the yeast to activate.

Make the filling: In a roasting pan, toss together the fennel and 2 tablespoons of the olive oil, breaking up any doubled-up fennel pieces with your hands. Season with kosher salt and black pepper and roast for 20 minutes, or until the fennel is nicely browned on one side. Add the tomatoes, sausages, garlic, chopped rosemary, and red pepper flakes, toss to combine, season again with kosher salt and black pepper, and drizzle with the remaining 2 tablespoons olive oil. Roast for another 25 to 30 minutes, until the tomatoes have totally collapsed and most of the liquid has evaporated. Stir in the preserved lemon peel and the parsley and transfer to a plate. Refrigerate the filling to cool it down while you form the dough.

After you put the vegetables in to roast, make the crust: In a medium bowl, whisk together 3 cups of the flour and the kosher salt, then add the yeast mixture and mix with a wooden spoon until all the liquid is incorporated and the dough forms a sticky mass. Transfer the dough to a clean work surface dusted liberally with flour, top the dough with flour, and knead until the dough is smooth, soft, and only a little tacky and cleans the board as you knead, adding flour as necessary, about 5 minutes. (You can also use a mixer: In the work bowl of a stand mixer fitted with the dough hook,

RECIPE CONTINUES ▸▸

1 preserved lemon, rinsed, quartered, flesh and pith removed and discarded, peel thinly sliced crosswise

¼ cup chopped fresh parsley

8 ounces store-bought vegan mozzarella cheese, such as Miyoko's or Violife; or homemade Easy Buffalo Mozzarella (page 235), cut into ½-inch cubes

TOPPING

Fresh baby rosemary sprigs (optional)

Flaky sea salt for topping

combine the flour and salt with brief pulses on low speed. With the mixer on the lowest setting, add the yeast mixture in a slow, steady stream, mixing until all the flour is incorporated. Add more flour, about 1 tablespoon at a time, until the dough cleans the sides and bottom of the bowl, then increase the speed to medium and knead for 3 minutes.)

Transfer the dough to a bowl brushed with oil, cover with a kitchen towel, and set near the oven (or in another warm place) to rise until roughly doubled in size, about 30 minutes. (You can make both the dough and the filling a day ahead: Let the filling come to room temperature, transfer to an airtight container, and refrigerate. Instead of transferring the dough to a bowl, transfer it to an oiled airtight container or zip-top bag and refrigerate. Proceed as directed, allowing the dough and filling to come up to room temperature before beginning and baking the calzones for about 5 minutes longer.)

Preheat the oven to 425°F. Line a sheet pan with aluminum foil, brush it with oil, and set aside.

Fill and bake the calzones: On a large, clean work surface or cutting board, divide the dough into four roughly equal pieces and roll each into a ball. (Scoop up any extra oil with the dough; it softens the crust of the calzones.) With a lightly oiled rolling pin or oiled hands, roll or stretch each piece into a roughly 8-inch round of even thickness. Transfer all four rounds to the prepared sheet pan, so that one half of each round is on the pan, the center of each round is on top of one long edge of the pan, and half of each round is flopping off the pan and onto the counter. (These wayward halves are the part of the dough you'll fold over your filling.) Pinch closed any holes that appear during the process. Pile about a quarter of the cooled filling onto the flat (supported) side of each dough round in a roughly half-moon shape, leaving a 1-inch border along the edge of the dough, then top each pile of filling with about a quarter of the chopped cheese. Stretch the empty dough halves over the filling and press, crimp, or twist to seal the two edges together to form a half-moon shape. (There are 101 ways to close a calzone—do whatever works for you that keeps the dough closed! And yes, it's fine if they touch.) Arrange a few tiny rosemary sprigs atop the calzones, then shower them with flaky sea salt. Bake for 30 minutes, or until golden brown, then brush each calzone generously with olive oil and bake for another 10 to 15 minutes, until the crust is deep golden brown and the filling just bubbles along the edge. Transfer the calzones to a cooling rack to rest for 15 minutes, then serve. (The calzones can also be cooled completely, covered, and refrigerated for up to 2 days, then reheated for about 20 minutes in a 350°F oven.)

Pambazos—A Guajillo Chile–Dipped Mexican Sandwich

Makes 8 sandwiches

At Miyoko's, there's always something delicious being cooked up in the staff kitchen where the chefs are hard at work preparing meals for all of our employees. One day, I was called into the kitchen to sample a special treat whipped up by Miguel, one of our kitchen staff and a former chef at a large Mexico City restaurant. I wandered in to find these strange, red, devilish-looking sandwiches that I had never seen or heard of before. "Pambazos," he told me. A popular street food in Mexico, pambazos are like a hot subway sandwich dipped in chile sauce and filled with a mixture of potatoes, chorizo, and cheese. Although I'd just had lunch and wasn't hungry, I had no problem chowing down the entire fat sandwich, wondering all the while how burritos established their place in American food culture, but these had not. I knew that it deserved a place in this book. Here's the recipe that Miguel taught me, including his excellent tomatillo salsa (but you can just buy a commercial version of the salsa if you like).

GUAJILLO DIPPING SAUCE

3 ounces dried guajillo chiles, tops removed

3½ cups water

½ teaspoon sea salt

FILLING

1 pound whole Yukon Gold potatoes

1 teaspoon sea salt

3 tablespoons neutral oil, such as sunflower, canola, avocado, or grapeseed; or vegan butter, such as Miyoko's

½ red, yellow, or white onion, diced

2 cloves garlic, minced

6 ounces vegan chorizo, such as Soyrizo or Upton's

Prepare the guajillo dipping sauce: Put the guajillo chiles and 3 cups of the water in a saucepan, bring to a boil, then turn down the heat and simmer for about 10 minutes. Transfer to a blender. Let the sauce cool to room temperature before blending in order to prevent splattering, or if you need to do it sooner, blend on low speed in small batches with the lid cracked. Blend until smooth. Strain through a sieve, adding the remaining ½ cup water to the sieve when mostly seeds remain to get the last bit of sauce to go through. Discard the seeds.

While the sauce is cooking, make the pambazo filling: Put the whole potatoes in a pot with water to cover, add the salt, and bring to a boil over high heat. Lower the heat and simmer until the potatoes are fork-tender, then turn off the heat. Remove the potatoes and allow them to rest briefly so they are cool enough to handle. Peel the potatoes and discard the peels.

Meanwhile, heat the oil or butter in a skillet over medium heat and cook the onion and garlic until soft, about 4 minutes. Add the chorizo and cook until browned, about 2 minutes. Add the potatoes to the skillet and mash with the chorizo well.

RECIPE CONTINUES ▶▶

TOMATILLO SALSA

4 ounces tomatillos, cut into quarters

2 ounces jalapeños (2 or 3 medium), tops and seeds removed

¼ white or yellow onion, diced

1 clove garlic, peeled

½ teaspoon sea salt

8 bolillo rolls (soft Mexican bread rolls—substitute soft sandwich rolls if you can't find them)

8 ounces vegan mozzarella or smoked mozzarella slices, such as Miyoko's, Violife, or Follow Your Heart; or homemade Easy Buffalo Mozzarella (page 235)

About 3 cups shredded lettuce

Prepare the tomatillo salsa: Put the tomatillos, jalapeños, onions, garlic, and salt in a blender and blend until the desired consistency is achieved. You can puree until smooth or leave it a little chunky.

Now you're ready to assemble the sandwiches: Preheat the oven to 400°F. Line a sheet pan with parchment paper.

Split a bolillo roll in half lengthwise as you would for a burger or sandwich. Remove the soft bread from the inside of the top half, making sure that you leave a perimeter of ½ inch or so. (Discard the removed insides of the bread or use it to make breadcrumbs.) Fill the cavity with the potato-chorizo mixture and top with the other half of the bread. Repeat until all of the sandwiches are filled. Now take a whole sandwich and carefully dip it into the guajillo sauce so that it is completely covered in the red sauce. Place on the prepared sheet pan and bake for about 10 minutes, until the sauce covering the sandwich is dry (this will also reheat the filling if it has been allowed to sit for a while).

To complete the sandwiches: Add a couple of slices of cheese, some shredded lettuce, and tomatillo salsa. Then gobble it all down while warm, and let it transport you to a balmy, noisy, life-filled street in Mexico City.

Puttanesca Tuna Melt

Makes 2 sandwiches

There is familiarity and comfort in a tuna melt, but there is rarely any sexiness—unless you swing it through the tradition of pasta puttanesca, a spicy, salty, and always-alluring Italian dish. (Alla puttanesca translates roughly to "in the style of a prostitute" in Italian.) The spaghetti version was supposedly so named because the ladies of yore cooked it to lure in customers. Or it was because it was something they could cook quickly between clients. Or (there are so many stories!) the flavor was said to mimic the women's personalities. In any case, the combination of tomatoes, capers, olives, spicy red pepper, and (traditionally) anchovies is certainly now an Italian staple. And those same addictive flavors, blended with fish-free tuna and a good vegan fish sauce standing in for the anchovies, make for a fast but killer dinner, mostly straight from the pantry.

2 teaspoons extra-virgin olive oil

1 large clove garlic, grated

½ teaspoon red pepper flakes

½ cup pitted kalamata olives, chopped

2 soft oil-packed sun-dried tomatoes, finely chopped

1 tablespoon drained capers, chopped

6 to 7 ounces vegan tuna, such as Good Catch or Jinka, unflavored, drained of any liquid

1 tablespoon pickled goathorn peppers, such as Mama Lil's, or other spicy pickled red peppers, finely chopped

2 teaspoons vegan fish sauce (see Glossary)

1 tablespoon chopped fresh basil leaves, or 1 teaspoon dried

Kosher salt and freshly ground black pepper

4 (½-inch-thick) slices hearty white bread

2 tablespoons vegan butter, such as Miyoko's, at room temperature

3 ounces vegan cheddar cheese, such as Miyoko's or Violife, sliced

In a small saucepan, heat the olive oil over medium heat until it shimmers. Add the garlic and red pepper flakes, stir, then add the olives, tomatoes, and capers and stir for about 1 minute, until the mixture begins to look dry. Transfer to a small bowl and add the tuna, goathorn peppers, fish sauce, and basil, then season with salt and black pepper. Set aside.

Heat a large cast-iron or nonstick skillet over medium-low heat. As the pan heats, prepare the bread by spreading one side of each piece with an even layer of the butter. Add 2 pieces of bread to the pan, buttered side down, then divide the cheese between the 2 slices and put half of the tuna mixture on top of each layer of cheese. Top with the remaining bread, buttered side up, and cook for 3 to 4 minutes, until browned. Carefully turn the sandwiches and brown for another 3 to 4 minutes, adjusting the heat as necessary, then transfer the sandwiches to plates and serve immediately.

Tonkatsu (Japanese Fried Pork Cutlets)

Serves 4

Tonkatsu, a thick pork cutlet that is breaded and deep-fried, was one of my favorite foods before I became a vegetarian at the age of twelve. Pork Tenderlove performs beautifully as a compassionate substitute for this. I always found it quite funny that in a world filled with a gazillion sauces, in Japan the one served with tonkatsu is referred to as simply "sauce." Sure, it can be called "tonkatsu sauce" as well, but usually it's just "sauce." You can buy bottles of this, a dark concoction that's salty, a bit tangy, with a hint of sweetness, made from soy, veggies, fruit, and sugar, at most Asian grocery stores or even online. If you can't find it, you can always substitute a mixture of ketchup and soy sauce (at about a 2:1 ratio). In addition to the sauce, tonkatsu is typically served with shredded cabbage upon which you squirt more of the "sauce."

Another popular dish, called katsu-karei, is a piece of tonkatsu atop Japanese "curry rice" (see Japanese Beef Curry, page 150). It is the ultimate comfort food served with a good dose of rice. For this, definitely forego the "sauce"! (If you make this, omit the beef in the curry and stick with just the veggies.)

1 cup all-purpose flour

1 cup water

¼ cup ground flaxseed

About 2 cups panko breadcrumbs

1 pound Pork Tenderlove (page 199) fillets, about ½ inch thick

Neutral oil for frying, such as sunflower, canola, avocado, or grapeseed

About ½ cup tonkatsu sauce

About 4 cups shredded cabbage

Cooked medium or short-grain white rice for serving

Have three bowls ready: Put the flour in one bowl. In the second, combine the water and flaxseed and whisk well to make a vegan "egg." In the third, put the panko. Take a piece of the Pork Tenderlove and dredge it in the flour. Next, dip the fillet in the flaxseed mixture, then coat it thoroughly in the panko. Pour oil into a deep fryer, wok, or pot to a depth of 2 inches and heat to 375°F. If you don't have a thermometer, you can test for readiness by taking a snippet of the Pork Tenderlove and dropping it in the oil. It should sizzle, sink to the bottom, and then immediately and steadily rise to the surface. If it lingers at the bottom, the temperature is too low and the tonkatsu will be oily; if it shoots straight up, the oil is too hot, so turn the heat down and allow it to cool momentarily. Fry the fillets, about 2 at a time so as not to crowd the pan and lower the temperature of the oil, until browned on one side, then flip to cook the other side. Drain on paper towels, and serve with "sauce," shredded cabbage, and rice.

Meat and Cheddar Pie
with Green Onion Biscuit Crust

Serves 6 to 8

A hearty dish where you get it all—savory ground vegan beef, cheddary goodness, and a flaky, fluffy biscuit topping with the twist of green onions and curry, adding another level of flavor. This is a great potluck dish or family-pleaser, served with a big green salad topped with juicy tomatoes.

FILLING

1 tablespoon olive oil

1 yellow or white onion, diced

2 cloves garlic, minced

Sea salt

12 ounces store-bought "raw" type vegan ground beef, such as Beyond Meat, Hungry Planet, Meatless Farm, Abbot's Butcher, Lightlife, or Sweet Earth; or precooked-style vegan ground beef, such as Gardein; or homemade Gluten- and Oil-Free Ground Beef Crumbles (page 195)

2 cups roasted or drained canned tomatoes

2 tablespoons tomato paste

1 tablespoon miso, any type

1 tablespoon soy sauce, tamari, or Bragg Liquid Aminos (see Glossary)

1 teaspoon dried basil

1 teaspoon dried thyme

1 teaspoon curry powder

½ teaspoon or more red pepper flakes

Freshly ground black pepper

8 ounces medium or sharp vegan cheddar cheese, such as Miyoko's, Violife, or Follow Your Heart, grated

Preheat the oven to 375°F.

Make the filling: Heat the olive oil in a deep skillet, add the onions and garlic, and sauté until translucent and tender, about 7 minutes. Sprinkle with salt and add the ground beef. If you are using the "raw" type, cook it according to the package instructions, usually until it browns or firms up. If using precooked-style crumbles, just heat. Add the tomatoes, tomato paste, miso, soy sauce, basil, thyme, curry powder, and red pepper flakes, season with salt and black pepper, bring to a simmer, and simmer for 5 to 10 minutes, until the tomatoes break down and all of the ingredients have melded into a lovely sauce. Transfer to a 9-inch round or square baking dish. Cover the meat with the grated cheese.

RECIPE CONTINUES ➤➤

BISCUIT TOPPING

2 cups all-purpose or whole wheat pastry flour

1½ tablespoons baking powder

1 teaspoon curry powder

1 teaspoon sugar

1 teaspoon sea salt

6 tablespoons neutral oil, such as sunflower, canola, avocado, or grapeseed; or vegan butter, such as Miyoko's, cut into ½-inch pieces

1½ cups sliced green onions or leeks (white and green parts)

1 cup unsweetened plain or "original" flavor soy, oat, or almond milk

Make the biscuit topping: Combine the flour, baking powder, curry powder, sugar, and salt in a bowl. Stir with a whisk to ensure everything is mixed well. If you are using liquid oil, simply add it and stir. If you are using butter, cut it in with a pastry knife to break it down into pea-size or smaller pieces. Mix in the green onions. Finally, add the milk and mix gently to form a dough.

Pile the biscuit mixture over the cheese and gently spread it to cover the filling completely. Bake for about 45 minutes, until nicely browned and crispy on top. Allow it to cool for a few minutes on the counter, then call the troops over to enjoy.

Meet the Animals

The combination of ground beef and cheddar is likely one of the stalwart combinations that define American cuisine. It surprises people when they learn that both could have come from the same cow. Angel, who came to Rancho Compasión as a calf, would have given milk yearly for four to six years, at which point she would have been "rendered" into cheap meat. (About 20 percent of the beef in the United States comes from retired dairy cows.) Luckily, Angel escaped that fate and has grown into the diva of the sanctuary. Every animal bows down to Her Grace and gets out of her way. She even has her own Royal Guardsman—Echo, the goose, who loves her to no end and follows her around wherever she goes. If you're a stranger and Echo doesn't know you, watch out! He will charge at you to protect his beloved Queen.

Weeknight Shepherd's Pie
with Bratwurst and Buttery Potatoes

Serves 6 to 8

I've stumbled upon a few pubs in the English countryside only to be surprised and delighted to see a vegan shepherd's pie on the menu, and I've ordered it each time. I think this quickie version stands up to all of the ones I've had. Made by topping a rich, meaty stew with buttery mashed potatoes, it brings warmth to a crowd on the coldest of wintry nights. This version, aromatic with the addition of mushrooms, thyme, and white wine, is lighter than most but still provides a huge dose of comfort with less than an hour's work in the kitchen.

Meet the Animals

I do have to tip my hat to England, which continues to evolve to become one of the most vegan-friendly places on the planet. Whether in London or the country, a vegan restaurant is a stone's throw away. Which brings me to Goober, a Berkshire pig, a breed that originated in nineteenth century England and is highly prized for its meat. At Rancho Compasión, Goober is prized for being simply lovable and goofy. The high-school girl who raised him as part of 4H fell in love with him and his sister, Gamber, and decided they deserved to live out their natural lives at a sanctuary instead of becoming bratwurst. Goober loves nothing more than a good belly rub, and at seven hundred pounds, you better watch out if he flops onto you by accident when he lies down so you can reach his belly better. And have you ever seen a large pig run? You should see Goober and Gamber run across the field when called!

2 pounds russet potatoes, peeled and cut into 1-inch pieces

9 tablespoons vegan butter, such as Miyoko's

2 medium leeks (white and light green parts only) halved and cut into ½-inch half-moons

Kosher salt and freshly ground black pepper

1 pound cremini mushrooms, trimmed and quartered

1 tablespoon chopped fresh thyme

1 clove garlic, chopped

1¼ cups dry white wine

2 cups vegetable broth

⅓ cup potato starch

¼ cup cold water

1 cup frozen peas

4 "raw" type vegan sausages, such as Brat Original Beyond Sausage, cut into ¾-inch coins

3 tablespoons nutritional yeast (see Glossary)

½ cup vegan sour cream, such as Kite Hill, Ripple, or Forager

Add about 1 inch of water to a large pot fitted with a steaming basket. Bring the water to a strong simmer, add the potatoes, cover, and steam for 12 to 15 minutes, until completely tender. Transfer the potatoes to a large bowl and allow to cool for 15 to 20 minutes while you make the stew.

Meanwhile, in a Dutch oven or other ovenproof vessel about 10 inches in diameter and 4 inches high, melt 2 tablespoons of the butter over medium heat. Add the leeks, season with salt and pepper, and cook, stirring occasionally, until the leeks have softened, about 5 minutes. Add the mushrooms, thyme, and garlic, season again with salt and pepper, and cook until the mushrooms have given up their liquid and begin to brown, about 10 minutes. Add 1 cup of the white wine and cook, stirring, until most of the liquid has evaporated, scraping the browned bits off the bottom of the pan, about 3 minutes (these browned bits help to color and flavor the stew). Stir in the broth and allow it to come to a boil. In a small bowl, whisk the potato starch with the cold water until smooth and immediately add the starch mixture to the pot. Cook, stirring occasionally, until the stew comes to a boil and thickens. Season with salt and pepper, then stir in the peas. Set aside.

Preheat the oven to 350°F.

While the vegetables cook, heat a large nonstick skillet over medium-high heat. Melt 1 tablespoon of the butter, then add the sausage, season with salt and pepper, and cook, stirring occasionally, for 5 minutes, or until the sausages are nicely browned. Add the remaining ¼ cup wine and cook, stirring, for 1 minute, or until most of the liquid is gone. Use a slotted spoon to transfer the sausage slices into the stew and stir to combine.

Add the nutritional yeast and the remaining 6 tablespoons butter to the potatoes, season with salt and pepper, and mash until fluffy and smooth. Stir in the sour cream and season with salt and pepper as needed. Pile the potatoes in heaps on top of the stew, so that the entire surface of the stew is covered, and smooth if desired. Bake for about 20 minutes, until the potatoes are browned on top. Remove from the oven and serve. (If you want to make it ahead, allow the stewy bottom portion of the pie and the potatoes to cool separately to room temperature, then cover and refrigerate separately for up to 3 days. Assemble and bake in a preheated 350°F oven for 40 to 50 minutes, until piping hot.)

Hominy and Carne Asada Enchiladas with Creamy Green Sauce

Serves 8

Try a new take on hearty, indulgent enchiladas by blanketing them in a rich, tangy green sauce inspired by the wet burritos of Southern California. The coconut milk lends the perfect creaminess to the sauce without overwhelming the other flavors, while seitan-based vegan meat gives just the right chewiness to counterbalance the creamy hominy. Add some vegan pepper jack cheese, which has a delicious deep spice on its own, and you've got a new house favorite. They're delicious with either chicken or beef, so take your pick!

For a more complex, spicier flavor, substitute poblano peppers for the bell peppers and increase the pickled jalapeños to 1 cup.

SAUCE

2 tablespoons extra-virgin olive oil

1 yellow onion, chopped

2 large green bell peppers, chopped

1 jalapeño, chopped

2 cloves garlic, chopped

Kosher salt and freshly ground black pepper

2 cups vegetable broth

1 bunch fresh cilantro (about 3 ounces), with stems, roughly chopped (about 2 cups packed chopped cilantro)

1 (13.5-ounce) can full-fat coconut milk

¾ cup pickled jalapeños (mild or hot) with their juices, or to taste

First, make the sauce: Heat a large high-sided skillet over medium heat. Add the olive oil, then the onion, and cook, stirring occasionally, until it begins to soften, about 3 minutes. Add the bell peppers, fresh jalapeño, and garlic, season with salt and black pepper, and cook for another 6 to 8 minutes, stirring occasionally, until all the peppers have lost their brightness and the onions begin to brown. Add the broth, cilantro, coconut milk, and pickled jalapeños, stir to combine, and bring to a boil. Reduce the heat to a simmer and cook for 15 to 20 minutes, stirring occasionally, until the cilantro has turned a darker shade of green. Using an immersion blender (or working carefully with a regular blender), puree the mixture into a smooth sauce. Transfer the sauce to a large, wide bowl, season with salt and black pepper, and set aside. (The sauce can be cooled to room temperature, covered, and refrigerated for up to 3 days. Bring back to room temperature before continuing, adding a touch of water to loosen the sauce if needed.)

ENCHILADAS

1 pound store-bought carne asada–style vegan beef or chicken chunks, thawed if frozen, such as Plant Ranch Carne Asada or Pollo Asada, prepared according to package instructions; or homemade beef or chicken, such as Charbroiled Succulent Steak (page 188; use 2 steaks), Not Mrs. Maisel's Brisket but Marvelous Nevertheless (page 192), Juicy Chicken (page 210), or Savory Roasted Chicken (page 212)

½ teaspoon ground cumin

Kosher salt and freshly ground black pepper

1 (15-ounce) can white hominy, rinsed and drained

12 ounces vegan pepper jack cheese, such as Miyoko's, or Monterey Jack–style cheese, such as Follow Your Heart or Violife, shredded or grated

16 (6-inch) corn tortillas

Vegan sour cream, such as Kite Hill, Ripple, or Forager, for serving

Chopped fresh cilantro for serving

Preheat the oven to 375°F.

Make the enchiladas: While the sauce is cooking, prepare the filling. Heat a large nonstick skillet over medium-high heat. Add the beef to the pan and season with the cumin, salt, and black pepper. Cook for about 3 minutes, until the beef is heated through and browned in spots. Transfer the beef to a bowl, stir in the hominy; when the sauce is done, add 1 cup of the sauce and about half of the cheese to the filling. Stir to combine.

Put the tortillas on a plate. Spread 1 cup of the sauce evenly across the bottom of each of two 9 by 13-inch baking pans. (You can also spread 2 cups in a roasting pan large enough to hold 16 enchiladas, if you prefer.) Working with one tortilla at a time, toast the tortillas over an open flame until browned in spots on both sides, about 30 seconds per side. (This prevents the enchiladas from getting mushy. If you don't have a gas stove, you can do this over a grill set to medium heat.) Place the tortilla on a clean work surface and spread about ¼ cup of the filling horizontally across the widest part of the tortilla. Roll the tortilla over the filling and transfer it gently to the pan, seam side down. Repeat with the remaining tortillas and filling, arranging 8 enchiladas in each pan (if using two pans). Drizzle the remaining sauce evenly over all the enchiladas, making sure you cover the edges of the tortillas so they don't dry out. Sprinkle with the remaining shredded cheese. (You can cover and refrigerate the enchiladas at this point for up to 4 hours before continuing.) Bake the enchiladas for 20 minutes, or until the cheese is touched with brown spots and the enchiladas are piping hot inside. (Refrigerated enchiladas will take 5 to 10 minutes longer.) Serve the enchiladas immediately (or they can sit for up to 30 minutes without losing too much heat), with sour cream and cilantro for topping.

Beer-Battered Fish and Chips

Serves 4

As a child, I remember driving to Sausalito, California, with my dad to get fish and chips at a little dive shop. The fish came in trays lined with newspaper to soak up the oil. In the new land of America that I had just immigrated to, this was the closest thing to all the fish I had grown up on in Japan, and it immediately became a favorite. In London, I've had vegan attempts at fish and chips made by simply wrapping tofu in nori, battering it up, and frying it—somehow, even in the best of British pubs, this missed the mark for me. The fish has to be somewhat flaky, which is why the jackfruit works well here. Of course, you can serve with tartar sauce, but for me, it's malt vinegar all the way, baby, that brings back those fond memories.

2 pounds baking potatoes, well-scrubbed (peeled or unpeeled, as desired)

2 tablespoons olive oil

1 teaspoon smoked paprika

Sea salt and freshly ground black pepper

8 ounces beer, preferably lager or pilsner

Pinch of baking soda

1 cup all-purpose flour

Neutral oil, such as sunflower, canola, avocado, or grapeseed, for frying

8 fillets Jackfruit Fish (page 232)

Malt vinegar for serving

Preheat the oven to 450°F. Line a sheet pan with parchment paper.

Start with the fries, as they will take 20 to 30 minutes to bake. Cut the potatoes into wedges or French fry shapes. Spread them on the prepared sheet pan, drizzle with the olive oil, and sprinkle with the smoked paprika. Season with salt and pepper. Toss to coat well. Bake until they are crispy, browned, and fork-tender.

While the French fries (the "chips") are baking, make the batter for the fish and fry: Pour the beer into a medium bowl and add ½ teaspoon salt and the baking soda. Whisk in the flour. Heat the oil in a deep fryer, wok, or pot, making sure you have at least 2 inches in there. When the oil reaches 360°F, dip the pieces of fish in the batter to coat well and fry, making sure not to crowd the pan, until they are golden brown on one side, about 3 minutes, then flip and cook until the other side is browned. Drain well on paper towels. For the full experience, serve the fish alongside the chips in a paper boat lined with newspaper, or just do what most people would do and use a plate. Serve with the malt vinegar for sprinkling or dipping.

CHAPTER 3

Weeknight Wonders

I'm often asked whether I ever cook anymore because I'm so busy running a company. It's a funny question to me, because I feel like it runs in my blood. It is how I unwind when I come home from work. It wasn't always that way. For years, like many parents, putting dinner on the table for the family was a stressful event. Don't get me wrong—I loved to cook. But I didn't like having to cook under pressure and satisfy everyone's unique needs in thirty minutes or less.

Luckily, I am at a place in my life now where I no longer feel the stress of needing to get dinner on the table or suffer the wrath of screaming kids. I can now pour myself a glass of wine, put on some music, and go into my zone where I shut out all of life's disturbances and begin the process of de-stressing. I start pulling random things out of my fridge, much of the time without a plan, ready to see where inspiration takes me that night. Still, as much as I love cooking, I usually get home from work late and don't need to undergo a three-hour cooking meditation. Time is still of the essence, even if it's just for your grateful spouse and yourself. The recipes here are either quick—thirty minutes or less—or might take longer but require so little hands-on time that you can relax or help the kids with their homework while dinner cooks itself.

Southwest Chicken and Corn Chowder

Serves 6 to 8

We need to talk about how you're treating your corn on the cob. No, it's not the way you cook it. (I trust you know already that it shouldn't be boiled for hours.) It's that when you cut it off the cob, for soups and salads and all that, you're missing the best part: the sweet, milky root of each kernel, which, when scraped off the cob with the dull side of a knife, yields a vegetal cream that adds body and texture and incredible flavor to, say, a chowder studded with poblano peppers, tomatillos, potatoes, and vegan chicken. In fact, it obliterates any need for thickeners, so there's no starchy blanket covering the flavors of the other vegetables. Try it here, and you'll never waste it again.

Use Plant Ranch's Pollo Asada or No Evil vegan chicken (like "Comrade Cluck") if you want to simulate dark chicken meat, or Tofurky or Gardein vegan chicken breasts if you want something whiter and less toothsome.

2 large poblano peppers
(about 12 ounces)

6 medium tomatillos (about 12 ounces), husks removed, rinsed well

3 tablespoons extra-virgin olive oil

1 large leek (white and light green parts only) quartered lengthwise, then cut crosswise into ¼-inch pieces

3 large stalks celery, cut into ¼-inch pieces (about 1 cup)

2 teaspoons finely chopped fresh oregano

Kosher salt and freshly ground black pepper

2 teaspoons Old Bay seasoning

6 cups vegetable broth

1 pound Yukon Gold potatoes (or similar), scrubbed and cut into ½-inch cubes

Working over a gas flame, toast the poblanos on a wire rack balanced above the flame until blistered and blackened all over, turning them with tongs as needed, 5 to 7 minutes total. Transfer the peppers to a large bowl, cover tightly with plastic wrap (or seal them in a large plastic container), and set aside. Repeat with the tomatillos, roasting and turning them for 3 to 4 minutes, then add them to the vessel with the peppers and re-cover. Set aside. (You can also blacken the vegetables by placing them on a rack in the oven about 3 inches below a preheated broiler for 4 to 5 minutes, rotating them every minute or so.)

Heat a large soup pot or Dutch oven over medium heat. Add 2 tablespoons of the olive oil and the leeks and cook, stirring occasionally, until soft and browned in spots, about 3 minutes. Add the celery and oregano, season with salt and black pepper, and cook for another 3 minutes. Stir in the Old Bay until it coats all the vegetables, then add the broth and potatoes and bring to a simmer. Cook for about 10 minutes at a low simmer, until the potatoes are completely tender. Mash the mixture with a potato masher a few times to break some of the potatoes up into smaller pieces.

RECIPE CONTINUES ▸▸

4 ears white corn, shucked

10 ounces store-bought vegan chicken, such as Plant Ranch, No Evil, Tofurky, or Gardein, thawed enough to cut if frozen; or homemade Juicy Chicken (page 210) or Savory Roasted Chicken (page 212), cut into roughly ½-inch cubes

¼ cup juice from a jar of pickled jalapeños, plus more to taste

½ cup vegan sour cream, such as Kite Hill, Ripple, or Forager

Chopped fresh cilantro for serving

Vegan oyster crackers for serving

Meanwhile, peel the skin off both the poblanos and the tomatillos. Seed, rinse, and chop the poblanos into ½-inch pieces and chop the tomatillos into roughly ½-inch pieces. Set aside.

Next, cut the corn off the cob. Working with one ear lying down on a cutting board, run a large knife along the cob the long way, cutting off a long strip of corn about 3 kernels wide. Rotate the cut section of corn away from the cutting board and cut off another strip. Repeat until all the corn has been cut off the cob. Now stand the corn up on the cutting board, and using the back (dull) side of the knife, scrape the cob vertically to release the remaining part of each kernel still lodged in the cob—you should get a tablespoon or two of milky business, and you want all of it. Repeat with the remaining 3 ears.

When the potatoes are done, add the poblanos, tomatillos, corn, and corn milk to the pot, stir to blend, and cook for 5 minutes. Season the chowder with salt and black pepper. (If you want to make the chowder ahead, stop at this point, cool it to room temperature, and refrigerate for up to 3 days. Bring back to a simmer before continuing.)

Heat a small skillet over medium-high heat. Add the remaining 1 tablespoon olive oil, then the chicken (and any crumbly pieces), and season with salt and black pepper. Cook for about 5 minutes, stirring occasionally, until cooked through and browned on all sides. Add the jalapeño juice and cook for another minute or so, until most of the liquid has evaporated.

Remove the soup pot from the heat, stir in the chicken mixture, and let the soup sit for 5 minutes off the heat. Stir in the sour cream until well blended and creamy, then season with more pickled jalapeño juice, salt, and black pepper. Serve hot, with cilantro and vegan oyster crackers (most are vegan).

Note: If you have any leftover soup, it needs to be reheated gently so the chicken retains its shape (some vegan chicken will disintegrate if heated too much, while others will not). Bring the leftovers to room temperature for about an hour, if possible, then reheat over low heat, stirring occasionally.

Spanish Chorizo, Kale, and Chickpea Stew

Serves 4

Throughout much of Europe, the idea of fast food is anathema to the concept of enjoying a meal, which means that even when you're on the road, there's always a good lunch to be had. In France, you'll find highway pit stops selling beef bourguignon. You'll see Italian drivers enjoying handmade pasta next to gas pumps, and in rural Spain, you're just as likely to enjoy a bowl of chorizo stew laced with smoky pimentón de la Vera and a slice of Spanish tortilla (potato omelet). This is my vegan take on that chorizo stew, made with a combo of soy chorizo, kale, chickpeas, and sweet potatoes instead, my more compassionate version is a nutritional powerhouse. While a wider selection of vegan chorizo seems to be hitting the shelves, the kind that works the best for this is Soyrizo or something similar, as it leeches a spice-forward oil when sautéed, which lends a distinct red color and deep smoky flavor to the stew's broth.

3 tablespoons extra-virgin olive oil

1 small yellow or white onion, chopped

2 cloves garlic, finely chopped

1 (6-ounce) bunch lacinato or green kale, stems removed, chopped

Kosher salt and freshly ground black pepper

¾ teaspoon smoked Spanish paprika (pimentón de la Vera)

1 tablespoon tomato paste

½ teaspoon dried oregano

1 small sweet potato, peeled if desired, cut into ½-inch cubes

1 (15-ounce) can chickpeas, rinsed and drained

4 cups vegetable broth, plus more as needed

6 ounces vegan chorizo, such as Soyrizo

1 tablespoon sherry vinegar, plus more to taste

In a large, heavy soup pot, heat 2 tablespoons of the olive oil over medium heat until it shimmers. Add the onions and cook, stirring occasionally, for 3 minutes, or until they begin to soften. Add the garlic and cook another minute or so, stirring frequently, then add the kale and season with salt and pepper and the paprika. Cook, stirring occasionally, until the kale has wilted, about 5 minutes. Add the tomato paste and oregano and stir until the tomato paste coats the kale evenly. Add the sweet potato, chickpeas, and broth, bring to a simmer, then reduce the heat to low and cook at a simmer while you cook the chorizo.

In a large nonstick skillet, heat the remaining 1 tablespoon olive oil over medium-high heat until it shimmers. Squeeze the chorizo out of its plastic tube and into the pan in walnut-size blobs. They won't be sexy, but let them be what they are in the pan for about 3 minutes, until the chorizo is well browned on one side. Turn the chorizo gently, spread it out in a thin layer in the pan, and let it brown again without stirring, about 3 minutes. (The chorizo is naturally crumbly and will break up plenty in the soup; here, you just want it to brown nicely against the pan to give it some chew.) Slide the chorizo (and any oil that accumulates) into the stew and stir gently. Stir in the vinegar, then season with salt and pepper and additional vinegar as desired, add a little more broth if you like a soupier soup, and serve piping hot. You can let the soup cool to room temperature and refrigerate, covered, for up to 3 days before reheating and serving.

High-Protein Spicy Miso Ramen

Serves 4 generously

Like every good Japanese, I know my ramen. I grew up on it. Instant ramen was our Kraft macaroni and cheese. In Japan, real ramen—not the instant kind—can be lunch, a snack, or what you eat at a stall on a city street at midnight after a night of drinking.

So, let's be honest. This is not real ramen. I've broken all the rules, using trendy bean-based noodles (which means the recipe is gluten-free if you also use the tamari instead of soy sauce) and adding a south-of-the border spin with chorizo (or you can keep it tasting more traditionally Asian in flavor by using vegan ground beef). Because the noodles aren't made of wheat, there's no need to cook them separately—in they go with the broth and seasonings, and you can call everyone to dinner in fifteen minutes. Whether it's a cold winter night or 11 p.m. after a night of drinking, it'll be delicious.

8 cups vegan chicken broth, such as Better Than Bouillon

1 tablespoon soy sauce or tamari

5 ounces sliced white or cremini mushrooms (2 cups)

4 cups shredded or thinly sliced kale leaves or packed whole baby spinach leaves

8 ounces edamame spaghetti or black bean spaghetti (see Note)

2 tablespoons finely chopped garlic

6 ounces store-bought vegan chorizo, such as Soyrizo or Upton's; or ground beef, such as Lightlife, Gardein, or Beyond Meat (if using the "raw" type, precook in a skillet according to package instructions); or Homemade "Raw" Ground Beef (page 193) or Homemade Ground Chicken (page 218)

4 tablespoons white or chickpea miso

1 tablespoon Chinese chili garlic sauce or sriracha sauce

1 tablespoon toasted sesame oil

4 green onions (white and green parts), thinly sliced

Have everything ready to go because once you start cooking, it will be done in 15 minutes. In a large pot, bring the broth to a boil and add the soy sauce, mushrooms, kale (if you are using spinach, wait and add it at the end), and spaghetti. Simmer for about 5 minutes, then add the garlic and chorizo and simmer for another 2 to 3 minutes, until the noodles are al dente. Turn off the heat. Stir in the miso, chili sauce, and sesame oil. If you are using baby spinach, stir in the leaves now. Portion into four deep bowls and top with a sprinkling of green onions for garnish.

Note: If you can't find bean-based pasta you can substitute wheat noodles, but wheat noodles will thicken the broth and are not gluten-free.

Linguine with Lemon-Garlic Scallops and Herbs

Serves 4

Made with mushroom-based vegan scallops, a good squeeze of lemon, and tons of fresh soft herbs, this light, springy pasta dish isn't one that leaves you moored to the couch after dinner. And because you can prepare the scallops while you're waiting for the water to boil and sear them while the pasta cooks, it's great for weeknights—but also impressive enough for company. If you like a bit of heat, add a pinch or two of red pepper flakes to the pan when you add the garlic.

Kosher salt

1 pound linguine or other long pasta

About 1 pound (1 full recipe) Quick Buttery Scallops (page 230), cooked, removed from the heat and left in the pan

1 tablespoon lemon zest plus ¼ cup lemon juice (from 2 large lemons)

2 cloves garlic, grated

Freshly ground black pepper

4 tablespoons vegan butter, such as Miyoko's, cut into small pieces

1 packed cup roughly chopped mixed fresh soft herb leaves, such as dill, tarragon, chives, parsley, and tarragon

Bring a large pot of salted water to boil for the linguine. Add the pasta and cook according to the package instructions until just short of al dente, about 8 minutes. A few minutes into cooking, scoop out 1 cup of the pasta water and set it aside for the sauce.

When the pasta is almost done, add the reserved water to the pan with the scallops. Stir in the lemon zest and juice and the garlic and keep warm over low heat.

Drain the pasta and return it to the pot. Add the scallops and their sauce and stir for a few minutes over low heat, until each strand of pasta is coated with sauce and the liquid is almost gone. Season with salt and plenty of pepper, then toss in the butter and all but a small handful of the herbs and stir to blend. Transfer the pasta to four bowls, top with the remaining herbs, and serve piping hot.

Roasted Butternut Squash, Sausage, and Mozzarella Fettuccine

Serves 4

A good vegan mozzarella melts beautifully on a pizza, but unlike traditional mozzarella, it also melts well into a sauce. I love it tossed into an autumnal fettuccine with butternut squash and spicy sausage because the cheese coats each strand with flavor. For something even more striking with an added layer of flavor, try this with smoked mozzarella!

Kosher salt

1 (2-pound) butternut squash

2 tablespoons extra-virgin olive oil

2 teaspoons chopped fresh thyme

Freshly ground black pepper

1 pound fettuccine (or similar long pasta)

1 pound (4 links) vegan hot Italian sausage, such as Hot Italian Beyond Sausage

8 ounces store-bought fresh vegan mozzarella cheese or smoked mozzarella cheese, such as Miyoko's, or homemade Easy Buffalo Mozzarella (page 235), cut into ½-inch pieces

¼ cup roughly chopped fresh Italian parsley, plus more for serving

Preheat the oven to 425°F. Line a sheet pan with parchment paper.

Bring a large pot of salted water to boil for the pasta.

Peel and seed the squash, then cut it into ½-inch cubes (you should get about 4 cups) and transfer them to a bowl. Add the olive oil and thyme, season with salt and pepper, and toss to coat all the cubes evenly. Transfer the squash to the prepared sheet pan, spread into a single layer, and roast for 20 minutes or until browned and fork-tender, rotating the pan and stirring the squash about halfway through. Set aside.

When the water comes to a boil, cook the pasta to al dente according to package directions, 10 minutes or so. Drain, reserving 2 cups of the pasta water.

While the pasta cooks, heat a large nonstick skillet over medium-high heat. Add the sausage and cook, turning occasionally, for about 6 minutes, until the sausage is evenly browned on all sides and cooked through. Remove the pan from the heat. Transfer the sausages to a cutting board and slice them into ½-inch rounds.

Return the drained pasta to the pan, along with 1 cup of the reserved pasta water and the cheese. Toss well with tongs to blend, then when the cheese has almost melted, stir in the sausage, squash, and parsley, adding more of the reserved water if you want a saucier pasta. Season with salt and pepper. Serve hot, topped with additional parsley and pepper.

Spaghetti and Roasted Meat Sauce Dinner

Serves 4 to 6

While a sturdy, satisfying American-style spaghetti dinner is a cornerstone of most peoples' weeknight repertoires, most of them start by opening a jar. The kind I like most—a hearty, savory scratch sauce cooked slowly over a series of hours, with pauses for stirring and tasting—can seem a heavy lift at 5 p.m. on a Wednesday. This version capitalizes on your oven's reputation as a reliable babysitter. Start by loading all of the ingredients into a roasting pan (note the harissa, which adds depth and a touch of spice), then turn your focus to whatever else needs doing. While you're busy, the wine will reduce, the various tomatoes will soften and sweeten at different rates, and the herbs will release their flavors, leaving you with a deeply flavorful meal that mostly cooks itself (but leaves nary a splatter on the counter). It's not instant, but it requires very little of that most limited resource: your attention.

Meet the Animals

We once had a beautiful soul at the sanctuary named Ericka. She was a Holstein dairy cow with arthritis who was going to be slaughtered young because she wouldn't be able to stand long enough to give milk. She was kind to all Rancho Compasión, becoming the "big sis" to Angel, who was a motherless calf at the time, and good friends with Goober, the Berkshire pig. She was a gentle giant who would not have hurt anybody. In her few short years at the sanctuary, she would run exuberantly down hillsides, expressing a joie de vivre that was a delight to watch. She was an ambassador for all farmed animals. Unfortunately, her body finally gave way to severe crippling. To this day, we miss this beautiful lady.

¼ cup extra-virgin olive oil

1 (28-ounce) can whole peeled San Marzano tomatoes

1 (28-ounce) can crushed San Marzano tomatoes

1 small yellow or white onion, quartered lengthwise and thinly sliced

1 carrot, diced

1 stalk celery, diced

5 cloves garlic, peeled and smashed

¼ cup torn fresh basil leaves (from 3 large stems), plus more for serving

3 sprigs fresh oregano

3 sprigs fresh thyme

1 tablespoon harissa, or to taste

1 teaspoon kosher salt, plus more for seasoning

Freshly ground black pepper

2 cups dry red wine

12 ounces store-bought precooked-style vegan ground beef, such as Gardein or Beyond Meat crumbles; 1 pound "raw" type vegan ground beef, such as Abbot's Butcher, Beyond Meat, Sweet Earth, or Meatless Farms, cooked according to package instructions; or Homemade "Raw" Ground Beef (page 193)

1 pound spaghetti

Vegan Parmesan cheese, such as Violife or Follow Your Heart; or Homemade Hard Parmesan (page 236) or Quickie Nut Parm (page 177) for serving (optional)

Set an oven rack to the middle position and preheat the oven to 450°F.

Drizzle the olive oil on the bottom of a large (roughly 9 by 12-inch) heavy baking pan. Add the whole and crushed tomatoes, the onion, carrot, celery, garlic, basil, oregano, thyme, harissa, salt, and plenty of pepper. Drizzle the wine over everything, then mix and mash thoroughly to combine, using your hands to break up the tomatoes and separate the onion slices.

Roast the sauce for 1 hour. Stir and mash the sauce (if you prefer a smooth sauce, you can quickly blitz it with an immersion blender), then crumble in the meat and stir it in. Roast for another 30 minutes, or until the sauce is beginning to caramelize on the edges of the pan and has thickened considerably. Season with additional salt and pepper. (You can make the sauce ahead and let cool to room temperature, then either proceed or refrigerate, covered, for up to 3 days. Reheat for 10 to 15 minutes in a preheated 400°F oven before continuing.) Pick out and discard any noticeable herb stems.

About 20 minutes before serving, bring a large pot of salted water to a boil for the spaghetti. Cook the pasta to al dente according to the package directions, then drain and serve, loaded with the meat sauce. Garnish with basil and cheese.

Lasagna Roll-Ups with Ground Beef, Duxelles, and Sun-Dried Tomato Pesto

Serves 4 to 6

What are duxelles? Sounds fancy for sure, but they're just finely minced mushrooms. Duxelles add flavor that complements—or enhances—any vegan meat, elevating it to another stratosphere. Yes, this sounds fancy, but it's a simple foundation for a beautiful dish that will be on time to your weeknight dinner table. Of course, you can use cannelloni shells, but lasagna sheets are so much easier to fill. Just roll them up with the filling, schmear the pesto on top, and you're good to go, or you can heat them in the oven for a bit while you're helping your kids with their homework. It's a bit highbrow in flavor, but your sophisticated kids will love them. And if you're short on time, skip the sun-dried tomato pesto and reach for a jar of good marinara—open, heat, eat.

SUN-DRIED TOMATO PESTO

3 ounces sun-dried tomatoes, soaked in warm water for 15 minutes, or until soft

1 packed cup fresh basil leaves

¾ cup olive oil

⅓ cup raw walnuts

2 tablespoons nutritional yeast (see Glossary)

1 tablespoon white or chickpea miso

4 to 6 cloves garlic, peeled

ROLL-UPS

Sea salt

8 ounces lasagna noodles (6 to 12 noodles, depending on size)

8 ounces white or cremini mushrooms, cut or broken in half by hand

4 cloves garlic, roughly chopped

2 tablespoons olive oil, plus more for the pan

12 ounces store-bought vegan ground beef, such as Gardein, Hungry Planet, Beyond Meat, or Sweet Earth; or homemade Gluten- and Oil-Free Ground Beef Crumbles (page 195) or Homemade "Raw" Ground Beef (page 193)

Preheat the oven to 350°F.

Make the sun-dried tomato pesto: Drain the sun-dried tomatoes, then simply combine all the ingredients in a food processor and process until relatively smooth. (Note: If you would like your pesto to be more like a sauce, reserve a cup or so of the pasta cooking water and mix it into the pesto to achieve the desired consistency.)

Make the roll-ups: Bring a large pot of salted water to a boil. Add the lasagna noodles and cook until they are al dente according to the package instructions. Drain.

Meanwhile, start the filling. Put the mushrooms and garlic in a food processor and pulse until they are finely minced. Do not allow them to become mush. Heat the oil over medium heat in a large skillet and add the mushrooms and garlic. Sauté until they are browned, about 3 minutes, then add the ground beef, sage, and basil and cook until the meat is browned, about 3 minutes.

While the mushrooms and meat are cooking, combine the cashews and water in a high-speed blender and blend until a creamy, smooth cashew cream has been formed. Pour the cashew cream into the pan, add the wine and nutritional yeast, bring to a simmer, and simmer for about 2 minutes to thicken the sauce. Season with salt and pepper.

½ teaspoon dried sage

1 teaspoon dried basil

⅔ cup unsalted raw cashews

1¼ cups water

2 tablespoons white wine

1 tablespoon nutritional yeast
(see Glossary)

Freshly ground black pepper

Now it's time to fill and roll up the noodles. Put ¼ to ½ cup of the filling on a noodle (depending on the size of the noodle), spread the filling down the length of the noodle, and roll it up. Put the rolls in an oiled 9 by 13-inch baking dish, seam side down. Cover with aluminum foil and bake for 10 to 15 minutes, until they are piping hot. Serve with the sun-dried tomato pesto schmeared on top.

Kimchi Beef Bowl

Serves 4 to 6

This doesn't parade around as an authentic Korean dish, but it's a quick Asian-style answer to a midweek dinner crisis. Serve it over rice, quinoa, or another grain that will soak up its juicy sauce. It's a one-bowl solution that delivers savory flavors, freshness, and nutrients to your whole family.

1 tablespoon peanut, avocado, canola, or untoasted sesame oil

1 yellow or white onion, sliced

6 cloves garlic, minced

4 ounces fresh shiitake mushrooms (2 cups), stemmed and cut in half

8 ounces store-bought vegan beef or seitan strips, pieces, or fillets, such as Asatsu, No Evil, or Upton's; or homemade Charbroiled Succulent Steak slices (page 188)

½ cup kimchi

1 bunch garlic chives, chives, or flowering garlic, cut into 2-inch lengths

½ cup vegetable or mushroom broth

2 tablespoons soy sauce or tamari

1 tablespoon gochujang sauce

1 tablespoon toasted sesame oil

1 teaspoon sugar or maple syrup

Cooked rice or quinoa (1½ to 2 cups per person)

About 1½ cups shredded white or red cabbage

About 1½ cups mung bean sprouts

1 large avocado, sliced

½ cup thinly sliced purple daikon or watermelon radishes

Heat the oil in a wok or other skillet capable of high heat. Add the onion and garlic and stir-fry over high heat until the onion slices are wilted, about 3 minutes. Add the mushrooms and beef and continue to stir-fry until the mushrooms are wilted, about 2 minutes, then add the kimchi and chives and cook for another 30 seconds. In a small bowl, combine the broth, soy sauce, gochujang sauce, toasted sesame oil, and sugar and stir well. Pour the sauce into the wok and simmer for a minute to allow flavors to meld. Turn off the heat.

Get some fun bowls and fill them halfway with hot rice or quinoa. Pile on the kimchi beef, then top with the shredded cabbage, bean sprouts, avocado, and radishes. Make sure you put a couple of tablespoons of the yummy sauce on top of each so that it soaks into the rice. Get some chopsticks and dig in.

King Trumpet Mushroom Carnitas Tacos

Makes 8 (6-inch) or 16 (3-inch) tacos

There's a certain amount of ritual involved in buying tacos at a taco truck. First, there's the line. Then there's the wait, and you're never not starving. But it makes the dive in that much better: choosing the correct bottle of salsa (always the smoky chipotle one), spraying the lime, folding the edges over wayward cilantro and onions, eating until the red sauce snaking its way down your hand threatens your watchband. But what if I told you that you can do even better at home?

Start by cooking two batches of my recipe for King Trumpet Mushroom Pulled Pork, using the non-smoked method that calls for smoked paprika. Set it aside while you make a cheater version of slow-roasted salsa that has plenty of good charred flavor, then sear the pork again, carnitas-style, until the mushrooms become chewy and caramelized. (I add cashews for texture.) Then dig in. You won't miss the line, and you probably won't miss another veggie taco.

2 pounds king trumpet mushrooms, cooked in two batches according to King Trumpet Mushroom Pulled Pork (page 202) and set aside

1 cup raw cashews, roughly chopped

½ small white onion, finely chopped

½ cup roughly chopped fresh cilantro

8 (6-inch) or 16 (3-inch) corn tortillas, warmed or toasted over a flame

4 radishes, thinly sliced

1 lime, cut into wedges

Cheater Charred Chipotle Salsa (recipe follows) for serving

On a large cutting board, run through the mushrooms roughly with a knife to cut the strands into bite-size pieces. When you're ready to serve, return the pan with all of the mushroom "pork" to the stovetop over high heat. Cook until the mushrooms start to brown and crisp, stirring often, about 5 minutes. Add the cashews to the pan and cook for another minute or so, then set aside.

While the mushrooms cook, in a small bowl, combine the onion and cilantro and set aside.

To serve, divide the carnitas mixture among the tortillas and top with the onion mixture and radish slices. Serve with the lime wedges and salsa.

RECIPE CONTINUES ➤➤

Cheater Charred Chipotle Salsa

Makes 2 cups

Made by simply whirling together charred onions, fire-roasted canned tomatoes, and canned chipotle chiles, this salsa can be a fridge staple with very little work.

1 small yellow, white, or red onion, peeled and halved through the poles

1 (14-ounce) can fire-roasted tomatoes

2 chipotle chiles (from a can of chipotle chiles in adobo sauce)

¼ cup roughly chopped fresh cilantro

1 large clove garlic, smashed

¼ teaspoon kosher salt

Place a grate over a gas stove burner on high heat. Add the onion and cook until charred on all sides, about 10 minutes total, turning the onion with tongs and allowing the layers to separate naturally as you go. You want all the layers to be tinged with black. (Alternately, you can broil the onions on a sheet pan for about 5 minutes, turning and rearranging every minute or so, until all the pieces are charred.)

Transfer the onion to a blender with the tomatoes, chiles, cilantro, garlic, and salt. Whirl until well blended but leaving some texture, then transfer to a jar. Use immediately or cover and refrigerate for up to 1 week.

My Mother's Sake Chicken and Rice

Serves 4

This was my mother's signature dish. After we emigrated to the States, my mother felt compelled to start cooking with a lot of meat. She added a Japanese spin to chicken, infusing it with sake. She was also a master of paper-thin mushroom slices, and she would tolerate nothing short of perfection. (Don't worry. She won't know if you haven't mastered this.) I loved it until I became a vegetarian at the age of twelve and had to renounce it forever. But at last, it is back in my life! It's a simple dish that takes just minutes to prepare.

Full disclosure: Having made this a number of times, the quality of the chicken is critical here. If you can, use the homemade Juicy Chicken or Savory Roasted Chicken, as they truly have a superior flavor and texture to many commercial varieties.

2 tablespoons neutral oil, such as sunflower, canola, avocado, or grapeseed

1 pound homemade (preferred) Juicy Chicken (page 210) or Savory Roasted Chicken (page 212), cut into strips or left as breasts; or store-bought vegan chicken strips, such as Gardein, Tofurky, or No Evil, or Better Chew (either frozen or refrigerated)

1 pound white or cremini mushrooms, thinly sliced, or oyster mushrooms, torn by hand into smaller clumps

1½ cups Japanese sake

1 cup vegan chicken broth, such as Better Than Bouillon

1 tablespoon soy sauce or tamari

2 teaspoons arrowroot or cornstarch

Cooked rice, either white or brown, preferably short-grain, for serving

Heat the neutral oil in a skillet over medium heat, add the chicken pieces, and cook until lightly browned, about 5 minutes. Remove from the pan and set aside. Sauté the mushrooms in the same pan, covered, for about 5 minutes, until fully cooked. They don't need to brown, but they can, and they will release a bit of juice. Put the chicken back in the pan. Add 1¼ cups of the sake, the broth, and soy sauce, cover, and simmer for 7 to 8 minutes to allow the sake to mellow and the flavors to meld and infuse the chicken a bit. Dissolve the arrowroot in the remaining ¼ cup sake and add to the pan, stirring, until slightly thickened. Serve immediately—with rice, of course.

Portobello Mushrooms Stuffed with Pesto Chicken

Serves 4

This weeknight wonder takes just minutes of prep and will impress your family and friends with its seemingly fancy creativity. Juicy portobello mushrooms are stuffed with a simple mixture of vegan chicken tossed with pesto, either homemade or store-bought, topped with gooey cheese, then baked to become a savory delight.

4 large portobello mushrooms, stems removed (save to use in other dishes)

½ cup plus 2 tablespoons Homemade Cheesy Pesto Sauce (recipe follows), or store-bought vegan pesto

8 ounces store-bought vegan chicken strips or chunks, such as Gardein, Better Chew, Tofurky, or No Evil Foods; or homemade Juicy Chicken (page 210), Homemade Ground Chicken (page 218), or Savory Roasted Chicken (page 212)

1 red bell pepper, finely chopped

6 ounces vegan mozzarella cheese, such as Miyoko's or Violife, grated or sliced

Preheat the oven to 375°F. Grease a 9 by 13-inch baking dish.

Using a pastry brush, paint the outside (top) of the portobello mushrooms with a bit of the pesto. Place them top side down in the prepared baking dish.

If using chicken strips or breasts, cut into ½-inch chunks. In a medium bowl, combine the chicken, red bell pepper, and the remaining pesto. Mix well. Fill the mushrooms with this mixture.

Top each the mushroom with the cheese. Cover loosely with aluminum foil. Bake for about 20 minutes, then remove the foil and continue to bake for another 5 to 10 minutes, until the cheese is melted, the mushrooms are browned and juicy looking, and the inside is nice and hot.

Homemade Cheesy Pesto Sauce

Makes about 1 cup

Pesto would be vegan but for the cheese. Here, nutritional yeast and miso pair beautifully to create the umami normally delivered by Parmesan, adding a rich, cheesy note to this popular sauce.

4 cloves garlic, roughly chopped

1 tablespoon white or chickpea miso, or to taste

¼ cup raw pine nuts or walnuts

½ cup extra-virgin olive oil

2 cups packed fresh basil

2 tablespoons nutritional yeast (see Glossary)

Combine all of the ingredients in a food processor and process until finely chopped. It doesn't need to be smooth, unless you prefer it that way; I like a little texture. Alternatively, you can do this in a mortar and pestle: Start by pounding the garlic, miso, and nuts and drizzle in a bit of oil. Then pound in the basil and the rest of the oil, and finally, stir in the nooch. Store unused pesto in a jar with a layer of olive oil on top (to prevent oxidation) in the refrigerator for up to 2 weeks.

Italian Sausage Sheet-Pan Dinner

Serves 4

The rise of the sheet-pan dinner—one made by tossing a bunch of vegetables and perhaps a protein together on a sheet pan and shoving it all in the oven so you have time to do something else—has been primarily beneficial to meat eaters. But plant-based "raw" type sausages are ideal candidates as well, as long as you add the sausages near the end of cooking, so they don't have time to dry out. (Precooked-style vegan sausages are not recommended for this—you want the kind that will ooze fat while cooking.) Add this to your weekly rotation if you're looking for a meal that can be thrown together in less time than it takes the oven to heat: You dump potatoes, onions, whole mini bell peppers, grape tomatoes, and mushrooms on a sheet pan, drizzle the whole shebang with olive oil, and you're basically done. It gets brightness at the end from a splash of sherry vinegar and a shower of herbs. With a good loaf of bread, you've got dinner solved.

1 pound red fingerling potatoes (or similar), halved if large

1 small red onion, halved lengthwise and cut into ½-inch slices

1 pound mini bell peppers (about 12), any color

1 cup grape or baby tomatoes

1 pound cremini mushrooms, trimmed and halved

1 tablespoon packed fresh oregano leaves

¼ cup extra-virgin olive oil

Kosher salt and freshly ground black pepper

4 "raw" type vegan Italian sausages, such as Beyond Meat, Meatless Farm, or Lightlife

2 tablespoons sherry vinegar

1 tablespoon finely chopped fresh parsley or basil

Preheat the oven to 400°F.

Put the potatoes, onion, whole bell peppers, tomatoes, mushrooms, and oregano on the sheet pan and drizzle with the olive oil. Season with salt and pepper and toss to coat all the vegetables evenly, then spread them out on the pan and roast for 20 minutes, or until the potatoes are almost tender. Add the sausages, sprinkle everything with the vinegar, and roast for another 10 minutes, until the vegetables have browned and caramelized around the edges. Shower with the parsley and serve immediately.

Stovetop Beef or Chicken Parmigiana

Serves 6 to 8

Don't leave a platter of this vegan parmigiana in front of me, or I'll just keep eating it. This is one of my absolute favorite dishes, and it's been a true family-pleaser as well. Be sure to use a really good-quality store-bought vegan beef or chicken, such as Herbivorous Butcher. But of course, you will likely have homemade Charbroiled Succulent Steak, Tender Fillet of Beef, or Juicy Chicken in your freezer that would be perfect for this. By utilizing excellent-quality store-bought marinara or tomato sauce and doing it all in one large skillet on the stovetop, this is an easy weeknight dinner that will have everyone running to the table. Serve with a good dose of pasta, simply tossed with a bit of olive oil and salt, and a big salad. Buon appetito!

About 1 cup unbleached or whole wheat pastry flour for dredging

3 tablespoons ground flaxseed

1 cup water

About 2 cups panko breadcrumbs for coating

1½ pounds store-bought vegan "steak," such as Herbivorous Butcher; or homemade Charbroiled Succulent Steak (page 188), Marinated Tender Fillet of Beef (page 190), Juicy Chicken (page 210), or Savory Roasted Chicken (page 212), sliced ½ inch thick (8 steaks, 3 ounces each)

4 tablespoons olive oil, divided

4 cups excellent-quality marinara sauce, homemade or store-bought

6 ounces vegan mozzarella cheese, such as Miyoko's or Violife, grated or sliced

2 ounces store-bought vegan Parmesan cheese, such as Violife; or Homemade Hard Parmesan (page 236), grated, or Quickie Nut Parm (page 177), plus more for serving

12 ounces cooked fettuccine or pappardelle (fresh whole wheat, if possible)

Sea salt

Have three cereal or similar bowls ready. In one, place the flour. In another, mix the flaxseed and water, whisking well with a fork or wire whisk, to make a vegan "egg." Fill the third bowl with the panko breadcrumbs. Dip each slice of the steak in the flour, dredging to coat both sides, then dip in the flax mixture, then coat all sides with the panko. If the flax mixture becomes too goopy as you work with it, simply thin it out with a splash of water. Set the coated slices aside on a dry, clean plate.

Heat a large skillet for a minute or two. Add 2 tablespoons of the olive oil and heat again briefly. Add the steaks and cook over medium-low heat until nicely browned on both sides, about 3 minutes on each side. Turn the heat down to low and pour about ½ cup of the marinara sauce on top of each piece. Top each piece with mozzarella cheese and sprinkle Parmesan cheese on top. Cover with a lid and cook for about 10 minutes, until the cheese is melted.

To serve, toss some just-cooked pasta with the remaining 2 tablespoons olive oil and a sprinkling of salt. Put the pasta on plates and top each with Parmesan.

Beef Stroganoff

Serves 6

When visiting some Eastern European countries a few years ago, I was eager to try some authentic stroganoff and goulash in the new vegan establishments that are popping up all over. The difference between goulash and stroganoff was not that great, except for the addition of a bit of sour cream in the latter. Call it goulash or call it stroganoff—just call it "dinner" in less than 30 minutes.

1 ounce dried porcini mushrooms

1½ cups hot water or vegan beef broth, such as Better Than Bouillon

2 tablespoons vegan butter, such as Miyoko's, or neutral oil, such as sunflower, canola, avocado, or grapeseed

1 yellow or white onion, diced

3 cloves garlic, minced

1 pound cremini mushrooms, sliced

2 tablespoons all-purpose flour

¾ cup red wine

2 tablespoons soy sauce, tamari, or Bragg Liquid Aminos (see Glossary)

1 tablespoon red or white miso

8 to 10 ounces store-bought vegan beef strips or chunks (not ground), such as Better Chew Shredded Steak or Gardein Beef Tips or Strips; or homemade Charbroiled Succulent Steak (page 188) or Not Mrs. Maisel's Brisket but Marvelous Nevertheless (page 192), cut into strips or chunks

1 tablespoon Dijon mustard (optional)

1½ cups vegan sour cream, such as Kite Hill, Forager, or Good Karma; or 1 cup vegan cream cheese, such as Miyoko's

½ cup chopped fresh chives (optional)

Sea salt and freshly ground black pepper

About 8 cups cooked fettuccine or rice

Soak the dried porcini mushrooms in a bowl with the hot water for about 20 minutes to soften.

Melt the butter or heat the oil in a deep pan, add the onions, and sauté for 5 to 6 minutes, until tender. Add the garlic and mushrooms and cook until the mushrooms are slightly browned, 4 to 5 minutes. Sprinkle the flour over the mushrooms and cook for 1 minute, then add the porcini mushrooms and their soaking liquid, the red wine, soy sauce, and miso. Simmer for about 5 minutes to let the flavors meld and thicken, then add the beef and cook for about an additional 3 minutes to allow the flavors to penetrate the beef. Finally, stir in the mustard and sour cream to form a creamy sauce. Stir in the chives and season with salt and pepper to taste. Serve with noodles or rice.

CHAPTER 4

Wow Them

I do love entertaining. That is something everyone know about me. Ever since I moved out of my parents' house and got my own apartment, having friends over for a delicious repast that I have spent all day, or even several days, planning and preparing has been a huge joy. I don't want to just fill your belly, I want to have you giddy on food at the dinner table. I want the main dish to be the belle of the ball like Cinderella entering the palace. I want to tempt you to take another bite even when you're full *just because.*

Certainly, many other dishes in this book are also fit for entertaining. BBQ Stick-to-Your-Ribs with Pineapple Barbecue Sauce (page 201), Japanese Beef Curry (page 150), and even Portobello Mushrooms Stuffed with Pesto Chicken (page 103) are all crowd-pleasers and perfect for your next casual party or potluck. But the convivial dishes contained herein were made for entertaining, for bringing people around the table. They are big recipes, both in the quantity they make (a minimum of six servings, but more like eight to twelve) and execution, where you will throw yourself lovingly into the kitchen in order to create a meal that will have everyone smiling, chatting, and enjoying the best that life, family, and friendship have to offer.

Whether it's a classic French dish such as Coq au Vin (page 122) for a special dinner party or the zesty Zen Kabobs in Orange Soy Marinade (page 143) for a summer poolside fiesta, every recipe in this chapter has that "wow" factor. But just because you are going to perform on the culinary stage doesn't mean that you should be scared. I've thrown a few simple recipes in there (Hasselback Steak with Balsamic Chimichurri Sauce, page 124, and Leek, Chard, and Chicken Filo Roulade, page 146) to get you started, but think of the bigger recipes with multiple steps and ingredients as beautifully choreographed dance numbers consisting of a series of dance steps that anyone can do. After all, life is about lights, music—and food!

Boeuf Bourguignon

Serves 8 to 10

Ever since I read Julia Child's recipe for this classic dish over thirty years ago, I have been making my own vegan version. This has been one of my go-to dishes for big, festive occasions when I want to impress everyone who is suspect about how fabulous vegan cuisine can be. Boeuf bourguignon is a fancy name for beef stew, but that's because the French version *is* fancy. It's rich and potent with the red wine on which it builds its foundation. I've made giant pots of this and entertained all sorts of people who smack their lips and come back for more. Yes, it takes a bit of time to make, so it's worth making enough that you can share with all your favorite friends—this isn't something you'll whip up for a group of four (unless, of course, you want leftovers). So serve it at your next holiday party and wow your guests.

SAUCE

3 cups diced yellow or white onions

2 cups diced celery

2 cups diced carrots

3 tablespoons olive oil

6 ripe tomatoes, chopped

3 cups hearty red wine

1 head garlic, cloves peeled and sliced

12 dried shiitake mushrooms

2 ounces sliced white or cremini mushrooms (about 1 cup)

¼ cup soy sauce or tamari

3 tablespoons red, white, or chickpea miso

1 teaspoon dried rosemary

1 teaspoon dried thyme

7 to 8 cups vegetable broth

12 ounces carrots, cut into chunks

12 ounces white or cremini mushrooms, cut in half

12 ounces baby potatoes, cut in half

6 tablespoons olive oil

Make the sauce: In a large pot or Dutch oven over medium heat, sauté the diced onions, celery, and carrots in the oil until relatively tender, about 7 minutes. Add the tomatoes, wine, garlic, mushrooms, soy sauce, miso, rosemary, and thyme and bring to a boil. Add 7 cups of the broth and, when it has reached a second boil, cover, lower the heat, and simmer for 1 hour or longer, up to another 30 minutes, to concentrate. Taste and adjust the seasoning, adding more broth if the flavor is too strong or simmering it down longer to reduce and concentrate the flavor.

Meanwhile, preheat the oven to 425°F. Line a sheet pan with parchment paper.

Place the carrot chunks, mushrooms, and potato halves on the prepared sheet pan and toss with 2 tablespoons of the olive oil, then season with salt and pepper. Roast for about 25 minutes, until tender.

Set a colander over a bowl and pour the sauce mixture through it to strain the vegetables, collecting the sauce in the bowl. Press as much juice out of the vegetables as possible (these vegetables are highly flavorful and can be pureed and used to make "meatloaf," burgers, etc.). You should have about 6 cups of the strained sauce.

Heat the remaining 4 tablespoons olive oil in the sauce pot. Add the beef and cook until browned, about 5 minutes. Remove the meat and set aside. Now make the roux: Add the flour to the pot and cook, stirring, over low heat for 3 to 4 minutes, until it's a light nutty brown. Add the hot strained

Sea or kosher salt and freshly ground black pepper

24 ounces store-bought vegan beef chunks, strips, or vegan steak, such as Gardein or Herbivorous Butcher; or homemade Charbroiled Succulent Steak (page 188), cut into 1-inch chunks

⅔ cup all-purpose flour

12 ounces fresh or frozen petite peas

½ cup chopped fresh parsley

Crusty bread for serving and dunking

sauce and whisk well to incorporate. Cook, stirring with a wooden spoon, until thickened, which should happen within a couple of minutes. Add the roasted vegetables and cooked meat back to the pot and simmer for about 10 minutes. Finally, add the peas and cook for another minute or two (if using fresh peas instead of frozen, you may need to cook a tad bit longer). Serve in bowls sprinkled with a bit of parsley and chunks of bread for sopping up the delicious sauce.

Bouillabaisse

Serves 6 to 8

When I wrote *The Homemade Vegan Pantry*, I couldn't decide between including a recipe for cioppino or bouillabaisse, both of which are among my favorite soups. I chose cioppino, but luckily, I get to share my recipe for bouillabaisse in this book. While they both originated as hearty fisherman soups, bouillabaisse is even more complex with the accent of saffron and the garlicky rouille, a thick pesto made of bread, garlic, and olive oil. This version features the homemade "fish" and scallops recipes found in this book, making it even more special. You need nothing more than a salad for a memorable meal.

You can make bouillabaisse a day or two before you serve it, as it will develop even more flavor. Don't add the homemade fish, croutes, and rouille until serving time, however.

BOUILLABAISSE

¼ cup extra-virgin olive oil, plus more for frying the fish

1 yellow or white onion, diced

1 carrot, diced

1 fennel bulb, cored and diced

1 red bell pepper, diced

8 cloves garlic, minced

Sea salt

1 pound very ripe fresh tomatoes, diced, or 1 (15-ounce) can diced tomatoes

5 cups vegetable stock

½ cup white wine

1 sheet nori

Large pinch of saffron

2 or 3 dashes of cayenne pepper

2 medium Yukon Gold potatoes, cut into ½-inch cubes

8 ounces oyster mushrooms

8 ounces store-bought vegan shrimp, such as Sophie's Kitchen, Layonna, or Loving Hut

RECIPE CONTINUES ➻

Make the bouillabaisse: In a large Dutch oven or soup pot, heat the olive oil over medium, then add the onions, carrot, fennel, bell pepper, garlic, and a good pinch of salt and sauté for about 10 minutes, until the vegetables are tender. Add the tomatoes, stock, and wine. Crumple the piece of nori in your hand to form a wad and add it to the soup. Stir in the saffron and cayenne and simmer for about 10 minutes, until everything is breaking down and beginning to meld together. Remove 2 cups of the mixture, including as much of the nori wad as you can (don't worry if you can't get it all), put it in a blender, and blend briefly until it forms a textured slurry. Put this back into the soup.

Add the potatoes, oyster mushrooms, and shrimp. Simmer for another 10 to 15 minutes, until the potatoes are tender. If you are not serving the soup right away, allow it to cool and refrigerate until you are.

While the soup is simmering, prepare the croutes (toasted bread) and rouille: Preheat the oven to 325°F.

12 ounces Quick Buttery Scallops (page 230)

8 fillets Jackfruit Fish (page 232)

Freshly ground black pepper

About ½ cup all-purpose flour

¼ cup minced fresh parsley

CROUTES AND ROUILLE

1 baguette

4 tablespoons extra-virgin olive oil

3 to 4 tablespoons water

2 cloves garlic, peeled

Dash of cayenne pepper

Sea salt

To make the croutes: Cut the baguette into ½-inch slices, reserving a whole piece about 4 inches long. Brush about 1 tablespoon of the olive oil on the slices on one side, set on a sheet pan, and bake for about 20 minutes, until lightly toasted. Remove from the oven and set aside. These will go on the bottom of the soup bowl.

Now make the rouille: You can make this with a small food processor, an immersion blender, or the old-fashioned way in a mortar and pestle. Cut away the crust of the remaining 4-inch section of the baguette. If you have a small food processor, simply put the bread in the bowl of the processor and sprinkle the water over it. Let it sit for about 5 minutes, then add the garlic and cayenne and process for 1 minute. Finally, add the remaining 3 tablespoons olive oil and season with salt. (If you are using an immersion blender, put the bread in a bowl, moisten with the water, and let it sit for 5 minutes. Then add the garlic, cayenne, and olive oil and use the immersion blender to make a thick sauce. Season with salt. If using a mortar and pestle, follow the instructions for the blender methods, but use your strength to mash it all together.) Set aside.

About 15 minutes before you are ready to serve the soup, make sure you have your Quick Buttery Scallops and Jackfruit Fish ready. For the fish, lightly coat it in the flour and quickly pan-fry over medium heat in a couple of tablespoons of olive oil in a skillet until browned on both sides, about 3 minutes per side. Sprinkle with salt and pepper.

Now you are ready to assemble: Put 2 pieces of the croutes on the bottom of each soup bowl—you'll want large, wide bowls for this. Put a few pieces of the scallops and a piece of fish in each bowl. Pour a good ladleful of the soup on top. Add a generous teaspoon of the rouille on top and sprinkle each bowl with parsley. Serve immediately.

Confit of Chicken and Baby Potatoes with Braised Fennel and Cabbage

Serves 4 to 6

This is proof that butter makes everything better. Some vegan chicken drumsticks or breasts can be less than stellar, but cooking them slowly in fat makes them over-the-top indulgently fabulous. Paired with the luscious and smoky braised fennel and cabbage, this dish is a transformative experience. Break open a bottle of your best Bordeaux and have a meal fit for a king.

The confit chicken can be made alone without potatoes or the side vegetables to play a part in another dish, such as sandwiches, a pasta, or Cassoulet (page 119). Just follow the instructions for cooking the chicken without the potatoes.

CONFIT

¾ cup vegan butter, such as Miyoko's, melted

3 tablespoons olive oil

2 teaspoons coriander seeds

2 teaspoons black peppercorns

½ teaspoon sea salt

2 bay leaves

1 pound store-bought vegan chicken drumsticks, such as Be Leaf; or vegan chicken breasts, such as Be Leaf, Layonna, or Gardein; or homemade Juicy Chicken (page 210) or Savory Roasted Chicken (page 212)

1 pound baby potatoes, scrubbed well

BRAISED FENNEL AND CABBAGE

2 tablespoons olive oil

2 fennel bulbs, cored and thinly sliced

½ head savoy or green cabbage, cored and cut into 4 sections, then sliced ½ inch thick

¾ cup vegetable broth

2 to 3 ounces vegan smoked mozzarella, such as Miyoko's, or other smoked vegan cheese

Make the confit: Preheat the oven to 300°F.

In a 9-inch square or similar baking dish, combine the butter, olive oil, coriander seeds, peppercorns, sea salt, and bay leaves. Add the chicken and potatoes and toss to coat. Cover tightly with aluminum foil and bake for 1 to 1½ hours, until the potatoes are very tender and most of the butter has been absorbed.

Meanwhile, braise the fennel and cabbage: Heat a deep skillet over high heat and add the olive oil. Add the fennel and cabbage and cook, allowing it to wilt, brown slightly, caramelize, and stick a bit, about 8 minutes. Add the broth, cover, and turn the heat down to medium-low. Cook until very tender, about 10 minutes, then add the smoked cheese, cover, and allow to melt.

Arrange the chicken, potatoes, and veggies on plates as beautifully as you can and pour yourself some of that well-deserved Bordeaux.

Chicken Breast Stuffed with Butternut Squash and Champagne Pomegranate Sauce

Serves 6

This is what you do when you have a bottle of champagne left over (if that ever happens). Or you can open a bottle just for this and drink the rest. Up to you. Do try to finish the whole bottle, though, if it's Dom Pérignon—or make this with lesser brands of champagne, like the annoying half-bottles of cheap champagne littering tables after your Uncle Tom's third wedding. If you don't have any bubbly, you can substitute a dry white wine, such as a Sauvignon Blanc. I've used a number of vegan chicken breasts (usually soy-based from Asia), and while some have been tasty, either my homemade Juicy Chicken or Savory Roasted Chicken is the best for this. Yuba, the skin that forms on soy milk, makes a convincing skin that not only holds everything together (or the stuffing would fall out) but is succulent and delicious.

STUFFING

1 pound peeled and diced butternut squash

1 yellow or white onion, finely diced

1 tablespoon olive oil

Sea salt and freshly ground black pepper

½ pomegranate, arils (seeds) only

CHICKEN BREASTS

6 store-bought vegan chicken breasts (5 ounces each), such as Gardein or Layonna; or homemade Juicy Chicken (page 210) or Savory Roasted Chicken (page 212)

1 or 2 large sheets frozen yuba (or fresh, if available; see Glossary)

¼ cup vegan butter, such as Miyoko's, or olive oil

¼ cup white wine

Start with the stuffing: Preheat the oven to 400°F. Line a sheet pan with parchment paper.

Combine the butternut squash and onions on the prepared sheet pan and drizzle on the olive oil. Sprinkle with salt and pepper and mix well. Spread into a single layer. Bake for about 30 minutes, until fork-tender. Remove from the oven and mix in the pomegranate arils. Turn down the oven temperature to 350°F.

Now stuff the chicken: Using a sharp knife, slice the chicken breast in half lengthwise, leaving it connected on one side so that it opens like a book. Stuff each breast with an equal amount of the butternut squash mixture. Run the frozen yuba under running water to make it pliable, then gently squeeze. Cut the yuba into six pieces, then wrap each breast in one. In a small saucepan, combine the butter, wine, and chicken base and heat until the butter is melted. If you are using a bouillon cube, smash it with a wooden spoon to help it dissolve as this mixture heats up. Place the chicken breasts in a lightly oiled 9 by 13-inch baking dish. Pour the butter-wine mixture over them. Cover the dish with aluminum foil and bake for 30 minutes. Pull the dish out of the oven and turn the breasts over.

RECIPE CONTINUES ➤

1 tablespoon vegan chicken base, such as Better Than Bouillon, or 2 vegan chicken bouillon cubes

CHAMPAGNE SAUCE

1 cup water

½ cup raw cashews

3 tablespoons vegan butter, such as Miyoko's

1 cup minced shallots

½ cup finely diced carrot

Sea salt

1 medium apple, cored and cut into ½-inch slices or chunks

2 white or cremini mushrooms, cut in half

2 cloves garlic, peeled

2 cups champagne

1½ cups vegan chicken broth or vegetable broth, such as Better Than Bouillon or homemade

1 teaspoon dried thyme

1 bay leaf

2 cups baby spinach

½ pomegranate, arils (seeds) only

Freshly ground white pepper

Remove the aluminum foil and bake for an additional 15 minutes, or until the skin has browned. Baste with the juices in the dish.

While the chicken is baking, make the sauce: Combine the water and cashews in a blender and blend for about 2 minutes, until smooth and creamy. Set it aside. In a deep pan, melt the butter, then add the shallots and carrots, sprinkle with a pinch of salt, cover, and sauté for 3 to 4 minutes, until tender. Add the apple, mushrooms, garlic, champagne, broth, thyme, and bay leaf and simmer without the cover for 25 to 30 minutes, until reduced by slightly more than half. Using a slotted spoon, remove and discard the apples, mushrooms, and bay leaf. (If you are not ready to continue the dish, set aside at this point while completing the other tasks.) Stir in the baby spinach, then add the cashew cream. Heat for a minute or two, until thickened. Finally, stir in the pomegranate arils. Pour over the baked chicken breasts and serve immediately.

Cassoulet

Serves 12

I don't want to scare you, as I want you to make this dish. But this French take on the ultimate comfort dish of beans and meat is not for the faint of heart. There is some serious meatiness to this, along with lots of fat, so this is not for those who fear butter. In addition to the butter, the other potentially scary thought is the numerous steps and ingredients, including some that are better prepared a few days in advance (or from your inventory of DIY meats in your freezer). If you are organized, you can make the whole dish in 3 to 4 hours, or you can make it in "parts" (such as cooking the beans and the confit oyster mushrooms) up to 3 days ahead. Please don't let the butter and time commitment scare you, as this is too good to pass up. It's a big dish for a big crowd, so gather everyone around and savor it. You needn't much more than a big salad and maybe a bit of crusty bread to serve with your cassoulet.

BEANS

1 pound large white beans, such as Tabais, corona, cannellini, flageolet, or great northern, soaked in water overnight

1 yellow onion, cut in half

2 whole carrots

2 stalks celery, cut in half

2 bay leaves

8 cloves garlic, peeled

1 teaspoon sea or kosher salt

OYSTER MUSHROOM CONFIT

¼ cup vegan butter, such as Miyoko's, melted

¼ cup olive oil

3 cloves garlic, peeled

½ teaspoon dried thyme

Sea salt

1 pound oyster mushrooms, torn into small clusters

Start with the beans: Drain the beans, place them in a large pot, and cover with plenty of fresh water. Add the onion, carrots, celery, bay leaves, garlic, and salt. Bring to a boil over high heat, then lower the heat and simmer for 1 to 1¼ hours, until the beans are almost tender. Do not overcook and allow them to turn to mush—the beans will continue to cook in the oven with the rest of the ingredients, so slightly al dente is fine.

While the beans are cooking, make the oyster mushroom confit: Preheat the oven to 300°F. In a 9-inch square or similar baking dish, combine the butter, olive oil, garlic, thyme, and a dash of sea salt. Add the oyster mushrooms, stir, and cover tightly with aluminum foil. Bake for about 50 minutes. The mushrooms will be tender, succulent, and lusciously rich. Set aside.

RECIPE CONTINUES ➻

RAGU

2 tablespoons olive oil

1 yellow onion, diced

1 carrot, diced

4 cloves garlic, minced

Sea salt

1 (28-ounce) can diced tomatoes

1 teaspoon dried thyme

Freshly ground black pepper

MEAT

1 pound Confit of Chicken (page 115, without the potatoes or veggies)

1 pound vegan sausage, such as Beyond Meat or Field Roast Smoked Apple Sage

12 ounces homemade Charbroiled Succulent Steak (page 188) or similar store-bought vegan steak, such as Herbivorous Butcher, cut into 1-inch pieces; or vegan beef chunks, such as Gardein

GARLIC BREADCRUMBS

¼ cup vegan butter, such as Miyoko's

4 cloves garlic, minced

2 cups panko or homemade bread crumbs

Now make the ragu: In a deep skillet, heat the olive oil over medium heat. Add the onion, carrot, garlic, and a dash of sea salt and sauté until tender, about 5 minutes. Add the tomatoes, thyme, and ½ teaspoon sea salt and simmer over medium-low heat for about 30 minutes, until thickened. Using a slotted spoon, add the beans and stir, then add enough bean cooking liquid to cover (3 to 4 cups). Add plenty of pepper and stir well.

Preheat the oven to 350°F.

While the ragu is cooking, prepare the meat: For the chicken confit, tear the meat off the drumsticks, if you used those. If your confit was made with breasts, slice or tear into strips or chunks. For the sausages, the preparation depends on the type you use. If using Beyond Sausage or the "raw" type, cook in a pan until browned, following package directions. Let cool, then slice ¼ inch thick. If using Field Roast or another ready-to-eat kind, simply slice. Toss all the meat together.

Now you're ready to assemble it all. Pour half of the bean mixture into a large roasting pan, then top it with the meat. Pour the remaining bean mixture on top of the meat, then spread the oyster mushroom confit (with all of its juices) on top of that. If you want to bake this later, cover and refrigerate for up to 6 hours.

Now, for the final touch, make the garlic breadcrumbs: Melt the butter in a skillet over medium heat and throw in the garlic. Stir in the breadcrumbs. Cook for about 1 minute to brown slightly, then spread the topping over the entire casserole. Bake, uncovered, for 1 hour (add another 20 minutes or so if refrigerated) until bubbly and hot. Serve immediately.

Coq au Vin

Serves 6 to 8

This drunken chicken stew with a bit of smokiness from the bacon or pancetta is a French chef's tribute to Dionysus, the god of wine. Like many other French classics, I could only taste them in my imagination as I worked my way through Julia Child's *Mastering the Art of French Cooking* in my twenties. Why? I had been a vegetarian since the age of twelve. What I wanted to learn were techniques that I could apply to vegetarian and vegan cuisine. I realized that the greatness of many of the classics really didn't depend on the meat, but its treatment, the sauces, the herbs, and spices— and oh, dare I say—the butter. Here, the vegan chicken (where the quality can differ greatly depending on the brand) undergoes a modified confit-style treatment, baked at a low temperature in a bath of butter and wine, rendering it tender, juicy, succulent, and worthy of starring in this glorious stew.

I don't think any former or even current meat eater would balk at a serving of this vegan rendition, even if he or she is French. It is crazy good. Be sure to have plenty of rice, potatoes, or buttered noodles such as fettuccine to serve alongside.

Meet the Animals

Because roosters don't lay eggs, they are more likely to end up as coq au vin early in life than egg-laying hens. One such rooster saved from that fate was Barry. Barry spent the first four months of his life in an aquarium before he was rescued by Farm Sanctuary and came to live at my animal sanctuary Rancho Compasión. Barry was a good, good rooster. We had another one named Miles who was not as nice, often attacking people. Whenever Barry saw Miles about to attack someone, Barry would chase him off. If Barry wasn't around, all I'd have to do was call his name and he would come running to protect me. May Barry live long in chicken heaven!

1¼ to 1½ pounds store-bought vegan chicken, whole or breasts, such as Be Leaf, Layonna, or Gardein; or homemade Juicy Chicken (page 210) or Savory Roasted Chicken (page 212)

¾ cup white wine

8 tablespoons vegan butter, such as Miyoko's, melted

2 teaspoons dried thyme

Sea salt

2 tablespoons olive oil

1 large yellow or white onion, sliced

8 ounces (3 to 4) carrots, sliced

1 tablespoon chopped garlic

8 ounces cremini mushrooms, thickly sliced

1¼ cups vegan chicken broth, such as Better Than Bouillon

2 cups red wine

¼ cup brandy or cognac

2 tablespoons tomato paste

6 ounces homemade Pancetta (page 208); or store-bought vegan bacon, such as Upton's, Sweet Earth, or Lightlife, diced (see Notes)

8 ounces pearl onions, fresh or frozen (see Notes)

Freshly ground black pepper

2 tablespoons all-purpose flour

½ cup chopped fresh parsley

Preheat the oven to 300°F.

If you are using a whole chicken, cut or tear it into large pieces about the size of a quarter or third of a breast. Combine the white wine, 6 tablespoons of the butter, 1 teaspoon of the thyme, and ½ teaspoon salt in a 9-inch square or similar baking dish and add the chicken. Toss well to coat, then cover the dish tightly with aluminum foil and bake for 45 minutes to 1 hour, until the chicken has absorbed most of the liquid in the pan and is juicy. You can prepare this up to 2 days ahead if you like.

Meanwhile, heat the olive oil in a Dutch oven or deep pan, add the onions, and sauté for 3 to 4 minutes, until they begin to wilt, then add the carrots and garlic and continue to sauté for about 10 minutes, until the onions are tender. If the mixture starts to stick, cover the pan to allow it to steam a bit. Add the mushrooms and cook for another 5 minutes, until they have wilted, then add the chicken broth, red wine, brandy, tomato paste, and the remaining 1 teaspoon thyme. Allow this mixture to come to a simmer, then add the baked chicken and all the juices in the dish, along with the Pancetta and pearl onions. Partially cover and simmer for about 30 minutes, until reduced by a third or so. Taste and season with salt and pepper as needed.

In a small bowl, mix the flour into the remaining 2 tablespoons butter and stir it into the pan. The liquid should thicken almost immediately and become a lovely sauce. Top with chopped parsley and serve.

Notes: If you are using Pancetta, all you need to do is dice it. If you are using store-bought bacon, you will first need to dice it and fry it in a little oil.

If you are using frozen pearl onions, you need do nothing special before adding them to the dish. If you are using fresh pearl onions, trim the tops, then blanch for a minute in boiling water to slip off the skins.

Hasselback Steak with Balsamic Chimichurri Sauce

Serves 6

Why limit the idea of Hasselback just to potatoes? If you have a stash of Charbroiled Succulent Steak (or a commercial vegan steak, such as Herbivorous Butcher) on hand, you can transform it into something that looks all-fancy but isn't. While this recipe is for 6 servings, it's easily pared down to make just one steak, so don't hold back because you have no one to celebrate with—make it a special one-person dinner if you're your favorite guest! And while rice, quinoa, or a baked potato would be great accompaniments, you could even go all the way and make Hasselback potatoes! Use the chimichurri sauce below or any store-bought chimichurri sauce. The one below is my attempt to deconstruct a local restaurant's chimichurri that I love. After missing the mark a few times, I finally figured out that the secret ingredient is a bit of aged balsamic vinegar, which is untraditional but adds a lovely touch of sweetness that balances everything else.

BALSAMIC CHIMICHURRI SAUCE
Makes 1½ cups

1 cup very finely chopped fresh parsley

⅓ cup very finely chopped fresh cilantro

¼ cup finely chopped red onion

¼ cup finely chopped red bell pepper

4 to 6 cloves garlic, finely chopped

1½ teaspoons dried oregano, or 1½ tablespoons fresh oregano

½ teaspoon red pepper flakes, or to taste

3 tablespoons red wine vinegar or lemon juice

1 tablespoon aged balsamic vinegar

1 cup extra-virgin olive oil

1 teaspoon sea salt

Freshly ground black pepper

STEAK

6 vegan steaks (4 to 6 ounces each), store-bought, such as Herbivorous Butcher; or homemade Charbroiled Succulent Steak (page 188)

Start by making the chimichurri sauce: Simply mix all of the ingredients for the sauce in a bowl and let sit at least 1 hour for the flavors to develop. If you don't like to chop or prefer the sauce not to be as loose, you can blitz it in the food processor for literally 2 or 3 seconds—just don't allow it to become a puree! It should be a loose sauce in which the individual ingredients are seen and sensed. The chimichurri sauce can be made ahead and kept in the refrigerator for 7 to 10 days to drizzle on just about everything.

While the chimichurri sauce is sitting and getting tasty, prepare the steaks. Preheat the oven to 350°F. Oil a 9 by 13-inch baking dish, or one big enough to fit all of the steaks without overlapping.

Find the sharpest knife in your drawer. (If it isn't sharp enough, sharpen it! Or use a mandoline.) Place the steaks on a cutting board and slice very thinly across as you would Hasselback potatoes (approximately ⅛ inch), almost down to the bottom but don't cut all the way through so that it stays together in one piece. Between each slice (or you can skip a slice every now and then if it's too much of a hassle), place a slice of tomato. If it is a large tomato, you may want to cut the slices smaller so they are not sticking out of the top of the steak too much. Transfer the steak to the prepared baking dish.

3 tomatoes, thinly sliced
(⅛ inch thick or so)

1½ cups very thinly sliced yellow, white, or red onion (use a mandoline if your knife skills aren't up to snuff— you want these really thin)

6 cloves garlic, minced

Sea salt and freshly ground black pepper

Olive oil for drizzling

Sprinkle the tops with the onion and garlic, then sprinkle them very lightly with salt and pepper. Drizzle with olive oil—about a teaspoon per steak should do the trick (feel free to add more if you have the need for lubrication). Cover the dish with aluminum foil and bake for 30 to 40 minutes, until the onions are tender and the tomatoes have wilted.

Carefully transfer to individual plates and top with the chimichurri sauce.

King Trumpet Pulled Pork and Leek Croquettes with Porcini Cheddar Sauce

Serves 6 (makes 12 croquettes)

I developed this recipe to serve at a high-end sporting event in the Napa Valley. The chef wanted a vegan menu option to serve guests who opted for meat-free. The people surrounding our group eating some ordinary-looking chicken dish kept looking wistfully at our plates and commenting how much more delicious our meal looked than theirs. This is a sophisticated version of what is known as korokke, a Japanese-style croquette usually made with potatoes and ground beef or vegetables and a favorite dish of just about everybody in Japan. Here, I've recreated them with "pulled pork," delivering comfort and elevated satisfaction at the same time. The slightly tangy cheese sauce complements and balances the richness of the croquettes. While these can be made bite-size and served as an appetizer, they are so good you'll want a good couple of them to dig your fork into, especially on a bed of wild rice accompanied by roasted Broccolini.

1 pound russet potatoes, peeled and quartered

Sea salt

¼ cup unsweetened plain or "original" flavor nondairy milk, such as oat, soy, or cashew milk

1 ounce dried porcini mushrooms, soaked in 4 cups warm water for 30 minutes

1 pound fresh ripe tomatoes, finely diced

½ cup red wine

12 ounces vegan sharp cheddar cheese, such as Miyoko's Farmhouse Cheddar or Violife, shredded, or cheddar cheese spread, such as Miyoko's Vegan Roadhouse Cheddah

Place the potatoes in a 1-quart saucepan and cover with water. Add a large pinch of salt, cover, and cook for about 25 minutes, until very soft. Drain well. Add the milk and mash well with a whisk. Set aside.

While the potatoes are cooking, combine the soaked mushrooms and soaking water, the tomatoes, red wine, and ¼ teaspoon salt in a 2-quart saucepan. Bring to a boil over high heat, then turn down the heat and simmer for about 30 minutes, until the tomatoes have fully broken down and the sauce has reduced by a third to half. Add the cheese and whisk until it melts and is fully incorporated. The sauce will thicken slightly as it heats. Cover and set aside.

RECIPE CONTINUES ➤➤

4 tablespoons vegan butter, such as Miyoko's

2 leeks, white and light green parts only, cut in half lengthwise and thinly sliced

12 ounces homemade King Trumpet Pulled Pork (preferred; page 127) or store-bought smoked vegan pulled pork, such as the Jackfruit Company, No Evil Foods, or Upton's

2 teaspoons chopped fresh thyme

1 teaspoon chopped fresh sage

Freshly ground black pepper

About 2 cups all-purpose flour

About 1 cup water

About 3 tablespoons ground flaxseed

3 to 4 cups panko or gluten-free breadcrumbs

Neutral oil, such as sunflower, canola, avocado, or grapeseed, for frying

Melt the butter in a large skillet over medium-low heat. Add the leeks and a pinch of salt and sauté for 7 to 8 minutes, until tender. Add the pulled pork, thyme, sage, and the mashed potatoes and mix well. Season with salt and pepper. Using an ice cream scooper, form 12 balls of the mixture on a sheet pan lined with parchment paper, cover, and place in the refrigerator to chill until firm enough to shape croquettes, at least 30 minutes.

When ready to form and fry the croquettes, get your coating station ready. Put the flour in one bowl and whisk the water and ground flaxseed together in another bowl to make a flax "egg." Put the breadcrumbs in a third bowl. Flatten the balls slightly to form ½- to ¾-inch-thick croquettes, then coat lightly in the flour. Dip them carefully into the flax egg, then coat in the breadcrumbs. If the flax egg becomes too goopy, simply add a few tablespoons of water to achieve the desired consistency.

Pour oil into a deep fryer, wok, or pot to a depth of 2 inches and heat it over medium-high heat to 375°F, or until a small piece of the croquette sinks when dropped in then immediately rises to the surface. Fry the croquettes in the oil for 2 to 3 minutes, then flip, and cook an additional 2 to 3 minutes, until golden brown on both sides, making sure not to crowd the pan—a good rule of thumb is to add only enough croquettes to the oil to cover half the surface area of the oil or less. Drain on paper towels.

Serve with a good helping of the porcini cheddar sauce.

Lobster Thermidor

Serves 4 to 6

I know. Lobster Thermidor is oh-so-1970s, when it was all the rage. But that doesn't mean that, like Formica, it's irrelevant now. It's still super yummy and actually really simple to make, especially if you've made the Loving Lobster ahead of time. You'll want a good-quality vegan cheddar and Parmesan for this, as the cheese is also an integral part of the dish, imparting flavor and richness.

3 tablespoons vegan butter, such as Miyoko's

1 tablespoon olive oil

½ cup minced shallots

Sea salt

6 ounces white or cremini mushrooms (2½ cups), thinly sliced

3 tablespoons all-purpose flour

2 cups Rich Homemade Cashew Milk (recipe follows), unsweetened plain or "original" flavor oat milk, or vegan half-and-half, warmed

3 tablespoons vermouth or white wine

5 to 6 ounces vegan medium sharp to sharp cheddar cheese, such as Miyoko's or Violife, shredded

Freshly ground white pepper

1¼ pounds Loving Lobster (page 227), cut or broken into pieces

2 ounces store-bought vegan Parmesan, such as Violife or Follow Your Heart; or Homemade Hard Parmesan (page 236), shredded or grated, or Quickie Nut Parm (page 177)

Preheat the oven to 350°F. Oil 4 to 6 ramekins or a 9 by 13-inch baking dish.

In a saucepan, melt the butter with the oil over medium-low heat, then add the shallots and a pinch of salt and cook for 3 to 4 minutes, until the shallots are soft. Add the mushrooms, turn up the heat to medium, and cook until the mushrooms are wilted, about 3 minutes. Sprinkle in the flour and cook, stirring, for 1 minute, then add the warm milk and stir with a wooden spoon until thick and smooth, about 2 minutes. Add the vermouth or white wine and 3 ounces of the cheddar cheese and cook until completely melted. Season with salt and white pepper. Stir in the Loving Lobster.

Distribute the Lobster Thermidor evenly among the prepared ramekins or pour it all into the baking dish. Combine the Parmesan and the remaining 2 to 3 ounces cheddar cheese and sprinkle it evenly on top. Cover with aluminum foil and bake for 20 to 30 minutes, until hot and bubbly and the cheese has melted, depending on the size of the dish and whether or not the Lobster Thermidor was allowed to cool before baking.

Variation

Extra Fancy Lobster Thermidor Vol-au-Vent (serves 4 to 6, or makes about 24 appetizers): This is even more oh-so-70s, perhaps, but it's a classic nevertheless. Pick up some frozen vegan puff pastry shells—either appetizer or entrée size—and bake according to the package instructions. Fill with the Lobster Thermidor, top with the cheese, and bake until the cheese is melted. Serve at a fancy party or for a holiday dinner.

Rich Homemade Cashew Milk

Makes about 2 cups

⅔ cup raw cashews

2 cups water

Combine the cashews and water in a blender and blend until smooth and creamy. This can be kept refrigerated in a jar for up to 4 days.

Garlic Lobster Fettuccine

Serves 4

We all love a good pasta dish but often think of it as something tasty but ordinary. Here's one that will have you swooning (but not sweating—it comes together in minutes if you have a stash of Loving Lobster tucked away in your freezer or fridge). Make sure you choose a good quality fettuccine and do not overcook it. The sauce is buttery but light with a hint of sweetness from the lobster and umami from the mushrooms.

1 cup water

½ cup raw cashews

Sea salt

8 tablespoons vegan butter, such as Miyoko's

1½ pounds Loving Lobster (page 227)

12 ounces white, cremini, chanterelle, or morel mushrooms, thinly sliced

2 tablespoons minced garlic

Freshly ground black or white pepper

12 ounces fresh fettuccine or 8 ounces dried

½ cup minced fresh parsley

As this dish comes together quickly, make sure everything is prepped and ready to go so as not to have a batch of mushy pasta. Start by making the cashew cream. Put the water and cashews into a blender and process until very smooth and creamy, 1 to 3 minutes, depending on the blender. Set this aside.

Put a large pot of salted water on the stove for the pasta and bring it to a boil, but don't cook the pasta before preparing the lobster sauce. The sauce will come together while the water comes to a boil.

In a deep sauté pan over medium heat, melt 2 tablespoons of the butter until it foams. Add the lobster pieces, give it a pinch of salt, and sauté gently for 4 to 5 minutes, until the pieces are hot and very lightly browned. Remove from the pan and set aside for a few minutes while you cook the mushrooms.

Melt the remaining 6 tablespoons butter in the pan over medium heat until it foams. Add the mushrooms and garlic and cook until the mushrooms are browned, about 5 minutes. Season with a bit of salt. Add the lobster back in and continue to cook for another minute. Set this aside while the pasta cooks.

Now turn your attention to the pasta. Cook the fettuccine according to the package instructions, making sure that it is perfectly al dente. You can err on the side of it being slightly chewy, as it will continue to cook in the sauce. (Mushy pasta won't do here, sorry.) Using tongs, scoop up the pasta and add it to the pan with the mushrooms and lobster (don't drain the pasta in a colander, in other words). Add approximately ¾ cup of the pasta cooking water and turn the heat back on under the pan to medium-low. Stir in the cashew cream and heat briefly until thickened into a lovely sauce, then mix in the parsley, season with salt and pepper, and serve immediately.

Beef Tamales with Mole

Makes about 16 tamales

I remember the first time I ever made tamales over twenty years ago. Guillermina, a wonderful employee of another food business I had, taught me how to make them (along with enchilada sauce, mole, and other wondrous things). What I thought then hasn't changed: I wished they would magically form themselves. They are indeed an exercise in patience—but worth it. In Mexico, women form these while they chat away with each other, which makes the time go by. So invite your family members to help you make these, spreading the simple cornmeal dough (masa) onto corn husks, then filling the dough with a boldly spiced mole beef mixture, and finally wrapping it all up before steaming them. No, it's not a weeknight meal, but it's not particularly taxing, either—and the big reveal when it's time to eat, as each guest opens the first corn husk to uncover the steaming tamale within, is worth all the effort. They're particularly lovely served as a celebratory food—for Christmas and other holidays—because they're so gift-like. There's plenty of mole sauce for serving, and you can keep any extra well sealed in the fridge for up to two weeks.

Look for corn husks in a Latin grocery store, or in the Mexican section of a well-stocked supermarket. Usually one package has many more than you'll need for this recipe, which will serve four to six people easily. If the corn husks you find aren't totally soft and pliable, soak them in a large bowl of the hottest tap water while you prepare everything else—you may need to weight them with a plate to keep them fully submerged.

As for the chiles, look for bright, pliable dried chiles; older chiles, which tend to darken with time, don't always hydrate fully.

RECIPE CONTINUES ➻

MOLE

6 dried guajillo chiles

6 dried California chiles

5 medium ripe tomatoes (about 1½ pounds), stems removed, halved through the equator

1 small yellow onion, quartered

3 tablespoons neutral oil, such as sunflower, canola, avocado, or grapeseed

1½ teaspoons dried Mexican oregano

Kosher salt and freshly ground black pepper

2 teaspoons cumin seeds

3 cloves garlic, roughly chopped

1 cup roasted unsalted hulled pumpkin seeds

2 ounces vegan dark chocolate, grated (about ½ cup packed), or ⅓ cup vegan dark chocolate chips

1 teaspoon ground cinnamon

1½ cups vegetable broth

Preheat the oven to 450°F.

Start the mole sauce: First, toast each chile for a few seconds over a high flame on the stove, using tongs to hold it about an inch from the flame, until it smokes or crackles and begins to brown. (This brings out a little more flavor in the chiles, but you can skip this step if you prefer.) Put the toasted chiles in a bowl and add boiling water to cover. (Add more water than you need, because you'll be scooping a bit of this water out in a while. You can weight them with a plate if they bob to the surface.) Let soften until the water reaches warm room temperature, about 1 hour.

In a roasting pan, toss the tomatoes and onion with 1 tablespoon of the oil and the oregano and season with salt and pepper. Roast for 30 minutes, or until the tomatoes are collapsing and the onions are soft. Transfer the tomato mixture (and any juices) to a blender.

While the vegetables roast, make the filling: In a large bowl, whisk together the soy sauce and liquid smoke. Add the shiitake and trumpet mushrooms and stir to coat evenly. Heat a large skillet over medium-high heat. Add the oil, then the mushroom mixture, season with salt and pepper, and cook, stirring occasionally, until the mushrooms have lost their water and have browned nicely, about 10 minutes. Add the carne asada, cinnamon, cumin, and cloves, stir, and cook for another 2 to 3 minutes, until the spices are well distributed. Add 1 cup of the chile-soaking water, stir until the pan is dry, season with salt and pepper, and set aside off the heat.

When the tomatoes are done, go back to the mole: Heat a small skillet over medium heat. Add the cumin seeds and cook, stirring or tossing, until they begin to smell fragrant, about 1 minute. Add the remaining 2 tablespoons oil and the garlic and cook for another 30 seconds or so, until the garlic begins to brown. Add the oil and spices to the blender, then add the pumpkin seeds, chocolate, cinnamon, and 2 teaspoons salt.

When the chiles are soft, remove the stems and transfer the chiles and seeds to the blender, dumping any excess water back into the bowl as you go. Whirl until totally smooth, stopping to scrape down the sides of the work bowl as needed. Add 1 cup of the mole into the filling and stir until all the meat and mushrooms are coated evenly. Transfer the mole to a medium saucepan, whisk in the broth, bring to a simmer, and season with salt and pepper. Remove from the heat and set aside.

FILLING

2 tablespoons soy sauce, tamari, or Bragg Liquid Aminos (see Glossary)

½ teaspoon liquid smoke (optional)

8 ounces fresh shiitake mushrooms, stems removed, halved, then cut into ¼-inch strips

8 ounces fresh king trumpet mushrooms, cut into ¼-inch slabs, slabs broken by hand into jagged 1-inch pieces

2 tablespoons neutral oil, such as sunflower, canola, avocado, or grapeseed

Kosher salt and freshly ground black pepper

1 (16-ounce) package vegan carne asada, such as Plant Ranch Carne Asada; or homemade Charbroiled Succulent Steak (page 188), chopped roughly

½ teaspoon ground cinnamon

½ teaspoon ground cumin

¼ teaspoon ground cloves

DOUGH

4 cups masa harina, such as Maseca brand

4 cups hot water

8 ounces vegan butter, such as Miyoko's, cubed

1 tablespoon baking powder

1 teaspoon kosher salt

24 dried corn husks, rinsed

Meanwhile, make the dough: In the work bowl of a stand mixer fitted with the paddle attachment, beat the masa harina and 3 cups of the hot water on low speed until blended. Add the butter, baking powder, and salt to the mixing bowl and beat until the dough starts to come together. On low speed, add the remaining 1 cup hot water in a slow, steady stream—the dough should become smooth, like a thin cookie dough. Increase the speed to medium-high and whip for about 30 seconds, until light.

To form the tamales, choose the 16 biggest corn husks. (If you soaked your husks, spread them out on dish towels and dry them a bit on the towels before beginning.) Rip a few of the remaining rejected husks into ½-inch-wide strips. (You'll use these to wrap the tamales to close them.) Working with 4 husks at a time, arrange the husks flat on a clean work surface so the tip of each triangle is closest to you. Plop a generous ¼ cup masa dough onto the widest part of each husk. Using the back of a spoon, spread the dough into a roughly 4- to 5-inch square across the fat part of each husk, leaving about 1 inch of empty space on the top and sides of each husk. (You may have more or less room for the dough, depending on the size of the husk. Each one will be a little different.) Add about ¼ cup of the beef filling onto each square of dough and arrange the filling in an even strip parallel to the long sides of the husk, leaving about ½ inch of masa untouched at the top and bottom. Working with one tamal at a time, fold the long sides of the husk together, so the batter touches and encloses the filling, then tuck one side of the husk under the other, like you're wrapping a present. Next, fold the skinny end of the husk up and over the seam side of the tamal and tie the whole package closed with one of the reserved husk strips. (Leave the remaining end open; this is the top of the tamal.) Don't tie too tightly—the dough will expand during cooking. Repeat with the remaining tamales, then with the remaining husks, dough, and filling.

Pour about 2 inches of water into a pot large enough to fit the tamales upright. Add a steamer basket, a vegetable steamer, or a few small heatproof bowls and a small plate to the bottom of a pan—anything that will allow the tamales to steam without touching the water. Place the tamales in, open ends up. (If needed, fill any extra space on the bottom of the pot with crumpled aluminum foil.) Steam for 1¼ hours, or until the husks peel away from the dough neatly, adding a bit more boiling water if the water level gets low. Remove the tamales and let them sit on a platter, covered with a dish towel, for 10 minutes before serving. Gently reheat the mole over low heat and serve with the tamales.

Mustard-Glazed Pork Tenderlove with Root Vegetable Puree and Garlic Beans

Serves 4

This is a composed dish with different elements that come together as a whole: the lovely Pork Tenderlove glazed in mustard sauce atop a root veggie puree and accompanied by garlicky beans. Served with a bit of something green (Broccolini, perhaps?), it's the kind of dish you'd get at an upscale restaurant. It's a good one for practicing your presentation skills.

To make it as simple as possible, I've used canned beans for this. You can, of course, use homecooked beans, which would likely make it even better.

PORK

1¼ pounds Pork Tenderlove (page 199), sliced ½ inch thick

¼ cup plus 2 tablespoons olive oil

¼ cup maple syrup

3 tablespoons soy sauce, tamari, or Bragg Liquid Aminos (see Glossary)

2 tablespoons whole grain mustard

1 teaspoon lemon zest

ROOT VEGETABLE PUREE

1 pound Yukon Gold potatoes, peeled and thickly sliced

6 ounces parsnips, peeled and thickly sliced

6 ounces turnips, peeled and thickly sliced

Sea salt

2 tablespoons vegan butter, such as Miyoko's

½ to ⅔ cup unsweetened plain or "original" flavor nondairy milk, preferably oat, cashew, or another rich milk

Freshly ground black pepper

Marinate the pork: In a dish wide enough to hold all of the Pork Tenderlove slices side by side, combine ¼ cup of the olive oil, the maple syrup, soy sauce, mustard, and lemon zest. Place the pork slices in the marinade, turning to cover. Cover the dish and let marinate in the refrigerator for at least 8 hours or up to 24 hours.

An hour or so before you plan to serve, make the root vegetable puree: Put the potatoes, parsnips, and turnips in a pot and cover with water. Add about ½ teaspoon salt, cover, and bring to a boil. Turn down the heat and cook for 10 to 15 minutes, until the vegetables are fork-tender. Drain the water. Add the butter and ½ cup milk, and using an immersion blender or whisk, puree or mash the mixture well until creamy, adding more milk if you'd like it more saucey. Season with salt and pepper.

Make the garlic beans: Simply empty the can, including the liquid, into a small pot or add the homecooked beans with their liquid. Add the garlic and liquid aminos and simmer for 5 to 10 minutes until the beans are flavorful and the garlic has mellowed. Stir in the chives.

Now cook the pork: Remove the pork from the marinade, letting the excess drip off and reserving the marinade. Heat a skillet over medium heat and add the remaining 2 tablespoons olive oil. Add the pork slices and cook until each side is browned, caramelized, and glistening, 3 or 4 minutes per side. Pour in the remaining marinade and let it sizzle for a minute, then turn off the heat.

GARLIC BEANS

1 (15-ounce) can cannellini or lima beans, or about 2 cups homecooked beans in their cooking liquid

4 cloves garlic, minced

1 tablespoon Bragg Liquid Aminos (see Glossary)

2 tablespoons chopped fresh chives

To serve, spoon some of the root vegetable puree on a plate and arrange the pork slices neatly across or on top of it. Put some beans neatly on the plate and serve.

Pork Tenderlove Stuffed with Onions, Leeks, and Apples

Serves 6

Succulent Pork Tenderlove is given special treatment here stuffed with a savory and sweet mix of onions and apples, then wrapped in Prosciutto. Surrounded by roasted baby potatoes, it's a new, kinder, tastier spin on a traditional meat-and-potatoes dinner.

4 tablespoons olive oil, plus more for the baking dish

1 yellow onion, diced

1 large leek, white and green parts, sliced

2 medium crisp apples, such as Fuji, Gala, or Jazz, cut into ½-inch pieces

2 teaspoons dried sage, or 3 tablespoons chopped fresh sage

Sea salt and freshly ground black pepper

2½ pounds Pork Tenderlove (page 199), formed into 6 pieces

About 12 sheets Prosciutto (page 207)

2 pounds baby potatoes, scrubbed well and cut in half

1 teaspoon smoked paprika

Preheat the oven to 375°F. Oil a 9 by 13-inch baking dish.

Heat 2 tablespoons of the oil in a large sauté pan or skillet over medium heat, then add the diced onion and leeks and cook for 5 to 6 minutes, until they are almost but not completely soft. Add the apples and continue to cook until the onions and leeks are tender, about 3 more minutes. Turn up the heat to high and let the bottom caramelize for a minute. Turn off the heat and stir in the sage. Season with salt and pepper.

Take a piece of the Pork Tenderlove and split it in half so that it opens up like a book but is still attached on one side. Stuff each piece generously with the onion-leek-apple mixture. Then take 2 sheets of Prosciutto and wrap each piece to enclose the filling and cover the pork. Place the pieces carefully in the prepared baking dish seam side down, leaving room between the pieces.

In a bowl, toss the baby potato halves with the remaining 2 tablespoons olive oil and the smoked paprika and season with salt and pepper. Spread them around the pieces of Pork Tenderlove (if there isn't adequate room in the dish, you can bake the potatoes separately). Cover the dish with aluminum foil and bake for about 1 hour, until the potatoes are fork-tender. Uncover and serve.

Brisket Roulade with Duxelles and Truffle Demi-Glace

Serves 8

This is a spectacular dish suitable for any special occasion. The brisket can be made either the day of or days before. Highly recommended for this dish is Not Mrs. Maisel's Brisket; unfortunately, I haven't found anything commercially available that has the right texture or flavor. The tender brisket is stuffed with luscious duxelles, then it's all enveloped in a delicious demi-glace scented with truffles. Indulge or go home.

DUXELLES FILLING

1½ pounds white or cremini mushrooms, quartered

2 tablespoons olive oil

1 cup minced shallots

2 cloves garlic, minced

3 tablespoons Madeira, sherry, or brandy

½ bunch parsley, minced

1 cup soft breadcrumbs

2 teaspoons white truffle oil

Sea salt and freshly ground black pepper

TRUFFLE DEMI-GLACE

1¼ cups red wine

½ cup mirin (see Glossary)

Juices from the mushrooms

⅓ cup soy sauce or tamari

2 tablespoons white truffle oil

6 cloves garlic, minced

3 tablespoons cornstarch

¼ cup water

BRISKET

1½ pounds Not Mrs. Maisel's Brisket but Marvelous Nonetheless (page 192)

3 tablespoons olive oil or vegan butter, such as Miyoko's

Make the duxelles filling: Put about 2 cups of the mushrooms into a food processor and pulse to finely mince but not puree. Remove the mushrooms to a bowl and repeat until all the mushrooms are done. Place about 1 cup of the minced mushrooms in a tea towel and, over a bowl, squeeze to extract as much juice as possible and render the mushrooms as dry as possible. Repeat with the remaining mushrooms. Set the mushroom juice you have collected aside for the sauce; you should have ½ to ¾ cup.

Heat the olive oil in a skillet over medium heat, add the shallots and garlic, and sauté for 3 to 4 minutes until tender. Add the squeezed mushrooms and sauté for about 10 minutes, until the mixture is lightly browned and looks dry. Sprinkle the mushrooms with the Madeira and cook for a minute to reduce the flavor of the alcohol. Mix in the parsley, breadcrumbs, and truffle oil and season with salt and pepper.

Preheat the oven to 350°F for the brisket. Line a sheet pan with parchment paper.

Make the demi-glace: Combine the red wine, mirin, mushroom juice, soy sauce, truffle oil, and garlic in a saucepan. Bring to a simmer and simmer for about 30 minutes, until reduced by almost half and extremely flavorful. In a small bowl, dissolve the cornstarch in the water and whisk into the pot to thicken slightly so that it coats the back of a spoon.

While the demi-glace is simmering, cook the brisket: Slice the brisket into fillets that are about ⅓ inch thick, 6 inches long, and 3 to 4 inches wide. In a large skillet, heat the oil over medium-high heat. Add the brisket and sear the fillets on both sides quickly, about a minute or two per side. Remove from the pan. Place about ¼ cup of the duxelles on the bottom of each fillet, then roll it up. Place the rolls on the prepared sheet pan and cover with aluminum foil. Bake for about 20 minutes, until hot. Pour 2 to 3 tablespoons of the demi-glace over each serving of brisket and enjoy immediately.

Cabbage Rolls Stuffed with Wild Rice, Caramelized Onions, and Porcini in a Red Wine Sauce

Serves 6 to 8

I thank Julia Child for much of my culinary education, and one of the tricks of the trade I learned from her was how to prepare cabbage for making cabbage rolls. Honestly, I just can't be bothered to do all that careful blanching of the individual leaves so they aren't too crisp or mushy. What an utter hassle. Julia says just freeze and thaw! The freezing renders the leaves pliable as if it had been boiled, and you can now just put your effort into making the delicious filling.

1 medium head green or savoy cabbage

1 cup wild rice

5½ cups room-temperature water

3 tablespoons olive oil

6 cups thinly sliced yellow or white onions (2 to 3)

Sea salt

6 tablespoons red wine, divided

1 ounce dried porcini mushrooms

1 cup hot water

1 pound store-bought "raw" type vegan ground beef, such as Beyond Meat, Hungry Planet, Sweet Earth, Meatless Farm, Abbot's Butcher; or Homemade "Raw" Ground Beef (page 193)

3 cloves garlic, minced

2 tablespoons soy sauce, tamari, or Bragg Liquid Aminos (see Glossary)

¾ cup raw cashews

Freshly ground black pepper

When dealing with the cabbage, you have a choice. You can carefully cut the bottom and carefully peel the leaves individually, then blanch them in boiling water until they are pliable (the traditional way), or you can take a hint from Julia (she knows) and just freeze the whole head for a couple of days. No work involved. Julia and I—we highly recommend this method. Just leave it in the freezer for at least 24 hours, preferably longer (up to a week). Then let it thaw—it might take up to 24 hours to fully defrost. To do this, just place it in a colander over a bowl and leave it on your kitchen counter. Seriously. This is the easier method. Once it's thawed, just cut the bottom off and the leaves will be pliable and peel off easily. But of course, blanching the individual leaves can also be done.

Once you have the cabbage sorted out, get started on cooking the wild rice and caramelizing the onions.

Put the wild rice into a medium saucepan with 4 cups of the room-temperature water. Cover the pot, bring to a boil over high heat, then reduce the heat to low and cook for about 1 hour, until the water has been absorbed and the rice is tender. (This can be done up to 4 days in advance.)

Meanwhile, get started on the onions. Heat a large skillet over medium heat and add 2 tablespoons of the olive oil. Heat for a moment, then add the onions and a sprinkling of salt. Turn the heat down to low and cook the onions for about 40 minutes, stirring occasionally, until they reduce by about three-quarters and are browned, tender, and sweet.

RECIPE CONTINUES ➻

RED WINE SAUCE

1½ cups vegetable broth

1 cup red wine

¼ cup tomato paste

3 tablespoons soy sauce or tamari

3 tablespoons mirin (see Glossary)

2 bay leaves

2 sprigs fresh thyme, or ½ teaspoon dried thyme

1 ounce dried porcini mushrooms (optional)

Some might stick to the pan; that's okay, because you are going to deglaze it with wine. Add 3 tablespoons of red wine to the onions to deglaze—this will lift off any stuck onions. Stir to combine the flavors, then transfer to a dish.

While all of this is happening, soak the porcini mushrooms in the hot water for 20 to 30 minutes. When the mushrooms are tender, remove and chop them into ½-inch pieces, reserving the soaking water.

In the same pan, heat the remaining 1 tablespoon olive oil over medium heat. Add the ground beef, garlic, and soy sauce and cook until browned and crumbly, about 5 minutes. Add the remaining 3 tablespoons red wine and mix. Turn off the heat.

Now combine all of the previous steps. To the ground beef, add the wild rice, caramelized onions, and porcini mushrooms and their soaking water and mix well. Season with salt and pepper.

Next, make the cashew béchamel. Combine the cashews and remaining 1½ cups room-temperature water in a blender and blend until smooth and a cream is formed. Put the cashew cream in a small pot and cook over low heat until thickened into a béchamel sauce. Pour this sauce into the rice-beef mixture and stir well. Adjust the seasoning if necessary.

Now you are ready to roll the cabbage leaves. Place 1 leaf on a cutting board and, using a sharp knife, carefully remove the stem. Repeat with all of the leaves until you get to the very small ones in the middle—reserve and use those for another dish. Place ½ cup of the filling right above the removed stem. Fold the bottom flaps over in a crisscross fashion, fold the sides in, then roll it up into—well, a cabbage roll. Place closely together in a deep pan. Repeat with the remaining leaves and filling. You should have about 12 rolls.

Make the red wine sauce (which actually becomes a sauce as it simmers with the cabbage rolls): Mix all of the ingredients for the sauce and pour it over the cabbage rolls. (If you are using the dried porcini for the sauce, there is no need to soak them first—simply add them to the sauce.) Cover the pan with a lid or aluminum foil and cook over medium-low heat for about 30 minutes, until the sauce has reduced to a thick glaze. Uncover and serve.

Zen Kabobs in Orange Soy Marinade

Serves 6 to 8

This might have been the all-time favorite at Now and Zen Bistro, the vegan restaurant I had in San Francisco in the early nineties. When we decided to refresh the menu and took it off, the "regulars" were irate. These were a favorite at outdoor fairs as well, where we would sell thousands, often to unwitting omnivores who thought it was chicken. Juicy, tender seitan soaks the citrusy, tangy marinade, which caramelizes beautifully on the grill. This does best if grilled or broiled over direct heat. For those who are gluten-free, see the Variation. The marinade can be made ahead of time and refrigerated for up to a week or frozen for several months.

SEITAN

1 cup water

1 tablespoon soy sauce, tamari, or Bragg Liquid Aminos (see Glossary)

1¼ to 1½ cups vital wheat gluten (see Glossary)

1 yellow, white, or red onion, sliced

1 carrot, sliced

2 stalks celery, sliced

2 teaspoons sea or kosher salt

ORANGE SOY MARINADE

12 ounces frozen orange juice concentrate

½ cup red wine vinegar

½ cup soy sauce or tamari

2 cups olive oil

6 large cloves garlic, peeled

7 tablespoons toasted sesame oil

VEGGIES FOR SKEWERING

About 8 cups thickly sliced onions, zucchini, eggplant, red bell peppers, mushrooms, cherry tomatoes, or whatever is in season for grilling

Start by preparing the seitan: Pour the water and soy sauce into a bowl. Add the wheat gluten and stir to form a soft dough. It should be soft but and pliable but not mushy, so start with 1¼ cups and increase to the full 1½ cups if it is mushy. This needs to be soft to create a spongy meat that will soak up the marinade, so don't add too much wheat gluten. Mixing is all that is required—*do not knead*! The idea is to keep it as tender as possible, unlike many seitan recipes that are designed to be chewy. Cut or tear it into 3 or 4 pieces.

Meanwhile, fill a very large pot a little more than halfway with water, add the onion, carrot, celery, and salt, and bring to a boil over high heat. Drop the seitan into the water, turn down the heat, and keep it on a simmer, not a rapid boil. Cook for about 1 hour, until the seitan, when sliced in half, is thoroughly cooked—you'll be able to tell by fine little air pockets that should be visible on the inside. Remove the seitan from the water and allow to cool. (Don't discard the boiling water—it will be a flavorful broth that is great for soups, gravy, etc.)

Meanwhile, make the marinade: Simply put all of the ingredients into a blender and blend on high speed until smooth—like the texture of a smoothie. Transfer to a large bowl and cover. Refrigerate until using.

RECIPE CONTINUES ➤➤

When the seitan is cool enough to handle, tear bite-size or larger chunks off and squeeze them well to remove excess water (this helps it absorb the marinade and make it super juicy). Put the pieces of seitan into the marinade. Cover and marinate in the refrigerator for at least 24 hours. You can refrigerate it in the marinade for a week or so, or freeze for longer periods.

When you are ready to cook, heat the grill. This is a dish that requires direct heat or a flame in order to caramelize the outside of the marinated seitan and get those succulent grill marks to maximize flavor. So if you are going to cook it inside, make sure that you use a stovetop grill and turn it up high.

Skewer the seitan with vegetable pieces of your choice, baste it all with the marinade, and grill for 6 to 10 minutes, turning once, until golden browned with a bit of char. Be patient—this is best when it's grilled to perfection with caramelization on the outside, not just heated up on the grill. Baste again after pulling the kabobs off the grill. Dig in.

Variation

Gluten-Free Kabobs: You can enjoy this even if you are gluten-free. Instead of the seitan, just freeze 2 pounds of medium to firm tofu for at least a week, even longer—up to a year, if you like. I usually keep tofu in the freezer for dishes such as this. You can freeze the tofu in the tub it comes in. Thaw overnight, then gently squeeze out all the water until the tofu is dry and light. Cut it into 1-inch chunks and marinate (substituting tamari for the soy sauce), skewer, and grill.

Leek, Chard, and Chicken Filo Roulade

Serves 6

This is an upscale version of spanakopita that marries vegan chicken, infused with flavor from simmering in broth and wine, with herb-scented greens and cheese. Take your pick of the cheeses you want to use, and you can have a slightly different version each time. It's a perfect dish for a potluck or picnic as it holds up well and can be enjoyed even at room temperature.

3 tablespoons olive oil

1 large leek, white part, cut in half lengthwise, washed, and sliced

1 pound Swiss chard or kale, stems removed and thinly sliced

Fronds from 1 bunch fresh dill, chopped

Sea salt and freshly ground black pepper

8 ounces store-bought vegan chicken chunks or strips, such as Better Chew or Gardein (the former is tastier for this dish); or homemade Juicy Chicken (page 210) or Savory Roasted Chicken (page 212)

1 cup vegan chicken broth, such as Better Than Bouillon

2 tablespoons white wine

1 teaspoon dried thyme

8 sheets filo dough

½ cup olive oil or melted vegan butter, such as Miyoko's, for brushing on the filo

4 ounces store-bought vegan mozzarella or pepper jack, such as Miyoko's; or feta cheese, such as Violife; or homemade Easy Buffalo Mozzarella (page 235)

3 ounces vegan herb or chive cheese wheel, such as Miyoko's Double Cream Classic Chive or Double Cream Garlic Herb, or Treeline Herb-Garlic

Preheat the oven to 350°F.

Heat 2 tablespoons of the olive oil in a deep skillet over medium heat, add the leek, and sauté until tender, 5 to 6 minutes. Increase the heat to high, add the chard, and cook 2 minutes, just until wilted. The chard needn't be completely soft, just wilted—overcooking will lead to it becoming a watery mess, which you won't want. Stir in the dill and season with salt and pepper.

Meanwhile, put the chicken, broth, wine, the remaining 1 tablespoon olive oil, and the thyme in a small pot and simmer over medium heat 10 to 15 minutes, until the chicken has absorbed most of the liquid.

Now get your filo dough ready. Put a clean towel down on a clean, dry counter or cutting board. Open the roll of filo dough so that it is spread out completely. Line a sheet pan with parchment paper and put a sheet of filo dough on it. Using a pastry brush, lightly brush the olive oil or melted butter over the sheet. Place another sheet of filo on top and brush lightly with olive oil or butter. Repeat until all the filo sheets have been used. Put away the remaining filo for another use.

Spread the chard mixture over most of the filo dough, leaving a 4-inch section of plain dough without chard at one of the shorter ends of the dough. Then neatly place the chicken in a strip down the middle of the chard mixture, widthwise across the philo. Next, put the both the mozzarella and the creamy cheese on top of the chicken, spreading the creamy cheese as well as you can. Now, very carefully, take the chard-filled end of the filo dough and bring it over the pile of chicken and cheese to enclose it, then continue rolling up the entire thing as carefully as you can. The plain end will add a few extra layers to the roll. Brush the entire roll with olive oil or melted butter.

Bake for about 1 hour, until golden brown. Slice and serve.

CHAPTER 5

Around the World in Eighteen Dishes

It's interesting how so many people tell me that their exploration with food only increases when they go vegan. Perhaps the thought of potential deprivation (I guarantee, there is none!) makes people uber-alert to new flavor opportunities. I know one thing for sure: What excites most vegans about traveling is the opportunity to have new culinary experiences. The very first thing that any proper vegan does when he or she steps foot in a new city, in a new country, is to look for restaurants, street stalls, pop-ups, or cafés that offer the flavors of the land sans the animal products. Happily, there are several apps to help us in the search wherever we go, the most popular of which is Happy Cow.

As I travel around the world, it is so exciting to see how many vegan establishments are cropping up. In Tokyo alone, there are over two hundred, and in Budapest, I made the trek to a distant vegan cheese shop and along the way passed not less than half a dozen vegan restaurants (yes, I had to pop in to peruse the menu or buy a little something to taste despite not being hungry!). Even in Turkey, I had the most delicious and succulent stuffed zucchini, which I've tried to replicate here with the more traditional addition of meat (vegan, of course). And certainly, in my favorite of all places, Italy, vegan food can be found everywhere.

In this chapter, we'll discover some of my favorite finds from around the world, whether from Italy, Vietnam, Greece, or China, and even a few places I haven't been. With the new meat alternatives, making vegan versions of traditional dishes has never been easier.

Japanese Beef Curry
(Lovingly Known as Curry Rice)

Serves 6 to 8

"Curry rice" is to Japanese what mac and cheese is to Americans. It's Japanese comfort food, loved by all ages, kids and adults. Curry rice shops abound, and you can have it with anything—beef, chicken, pork, or even fried pork ("katsu curry"). This is not Indian or Thai or anything remotely like the cuisines that originated curry, but a Japanese adaptation that is more like a curry-flavored gravy with vegetables and bits and pieces of meat. You can make it as spicy as you like, or you can keep it mild—either way, it's a balance of spicy and sweet, with the sweetness often coming from apples. The key is using Japanese-style curry powder, which is readily available in Asian grocery stores, the ethnic section of large supermarkets, and online. In Japan, people buy a curry-flavored "roux" in a box that melts and thickens a pot of simmered veggies, but it's just as easy to make it yourself and has far fewer unpronounceable ingredients. I must admit that sometimes I just get a yen for curry rice.

If you want a double comfort dish, try making this without the vegan beef and topping it instead with a slice of Tonkatsu, or deep-fried vegan pork (page 70). It'll then become what's known as katsu-karei, which is about as hearty, comforting, and satisfying as you can get.

6 tablespoons neutral oil, such as sunflower, canola, avocado, or grapeseed, divided, plus more if needed to cook the beef

2 yellow or white onions, diced

Sea salt

8 ounces white or cremini mushrooms, sliced

4 cups vegan beef stock or vegetable stock, such as Better Than Bouillon, or homemade

1 large apple, about 8 ounces, cored and cut into chunks (no need to peel)

3 tablespoons Japanese-style curry powder (sometimes called Oriental Curry Powder, such as made by S&B— the style of curry powder is important), or to taste

2 tablespoons soy sauce or tamari

2 tablespoons tomato paste

3 cloves garlic, peeled

12 ounces baby potatoes, left whole, or larger waxy potatoes, cut into ¾-inch cubes

8 ounces carrots, sliced ½ inch thick, or baby carrots, whole

12 ounces store-bought vegan beef tips or strips, such as Gardein or Herbivorous Butcher; or homemade Charbroiled Succulent Steak (page 188), cut into 1-inch chunks

½ cup all-purpose flour

About 8 cups (or more) cooked medium- or short-grain white or brown rice

In a large pot, heat 2 tablespoons of the oil over medium-low heat momentarily. Add the onions and a generous pinch of salt and cook, covered, until soft, about 7 minutes. Add the mushrooms and cook until the mushrooms are tender, another 3 to 4 minutes.

Meanwhile, in a blender, combine the stock, apple pieces, curry powder, soy sauce, tomato paste, and garlic and blend until pureed. Add this mixture to the pot, then add the potatoes and carrots. Partially cover and bring to a simmer, then cook over medium-low heat for 10 to 15 minutes, until the vegetables are tender.

While the curry base is cooking in the pot, prepare the beef: If you are using homemade Juicy Charbroiled Steak or a steak from the Herbivorous Butcher, you need to do nothing but cut it into chunks. If you are using Gardein, Beyond Meat, or another brand, follow the instructions on the package as to whether it should be sautéed prior to adding to a dish. If so, add a tablespoon of oil to a skillet and cook until browned.

The key to thickening the curry is the roux. Now it's time to make it. Heat the remaining 4 tablespoons oil in a small pot. Add the flour and cook, stirring with a wooden spoon, for 4 to 5 minutes, until the flour is slightly lighter in color. Add the roux into the pot of goodies and stir until the sauce is thick like gravy. Add the beef and heat briefly. Serve with lots of rice.

This keeps in the fridge for up to 4 days or it can be frozen for 3 months.

Variation

Oil-Free Curry Rice: Sauté the onions in a bit of water, covered, until tender. In order to thicken the curry, instead of the roux with oil and flour, sprinkle about ½ cup potato flour (not potato starch) into the pot and stir until dissolved and thickened; if you want it thicker, add more.

Sukiyaki

Serves 6

This is essentially the mother of one-pot dishes, dating back several hundreds of years in Japan, and it's as popular today as ever. All it needs is a bowl of rice to accompany the juicy ingredients pulled from the simmering pot. Traditionally, it's a communal dish—a burner is placed on the table with a wide ceramic pot set on top. First, the "beef" is sautéed to brown it. Then the other ingredients are added in neat little piles—tofu, eggplant, greens, mushrooms, and shirataki noodles—as much as will fit, and a sauce of soy sauce, sugar, and mirin is poured over them. The pot comes to a simmer, the ingredients become infused with the flavor of the sauce and cook down, and diners replenish the simmering pot with more ingredients as they eat from the pot. But the true star of the dish is the shirataki, a noodle made from konjac, a fibrous root. The amazing thing about shirataki noodles is that they have—get this—*no calories*! They also soak up the juices while cooking and become utterly delicious. Luckily, shirataki noodles, such as the Miracle Noodle brand, are now widely available in grocery stores (they are sold in bags in the refrigerated section, not dry on the shelf).

The quantities for all of the ingredients, except for the green onions, are very flexible. Add more, add less, or use different veggies than I've suggested.

SUKIYAKI

1 tablespoon neutral oil, such as sunflower, canola, avocado, or grapeseed

8 to 12 ounces store-bought vegan beef slices or chunks, such as Gardein or Herbivorous Butcher; or homemade Charbroiled Succulent Steak (page 188)

At least 1 pound shirataki noodles, drained and rinsed

12 ounces firm tofu, cut into ½-inch-thick slices

6 ounces fresh shiitake or oyster mushrooms, cut or torn in half (3 cups)

2 Japanese or Italian eggplants, sliced ½ inch thick

Make the sukiyaki: In a large, deep skillet or pan, heat the oil briefly over medium heat, then add the beef and cook until slightly browned, about 3 minutes. While the beef is cooking, put the shirataki noodles on a cutting board and cut them roughly just three or four times (the noodles are *very* long and will be difficult to eat if you do not cut them). Push the beef to one side of the pan, then add the tofu in a neat pile next to the beef, then the mushrooms, eggplant, shirataki noodles, and some of the cabbage, all in neat piles (as much as will fit—you can add more later).

Make the cooking sauce and finish the dish: In a small bowl, mix the soy sauce, mirin, and sugar and pour it over the ingredients in the pan. Cover the pan, bring to a simmer, and cook for 4 to 5 minutes, until the vegetables have reduced in size. The vegetables will release their juices and dilute the sauce so that it will be not only abundant in the pan but a perfect balance of sweet and salty. Add the green onions on top, cover

½ head napa cabbage, cut into big chunks

4 bunches green onions (white and green parts), cut into 3-inch lengths

1 tablespoon grated fresh ginger (not traditional, but good)

COOKING SAUCE

½ cup soy sauce

⅓ cup mirin (see Glossary)

¼ cup sugar

Cooked rice for serving

again, and simmer until the green onions and cabbage are tender, another minute or two. Add the ginger and stir just a bit so as not to disturb the neat piles you so carefully created.

Serve with rice, leaving some liquid in the pan and adding the remaining vegetables and noodles to simmer while you eat, so people can go back for seconds. Itadakimasu! ("Let's eat!" in Japanese.)

Chicken and Rice Cakes with Gai Lan and Shiitakes

Serves 4

Frequently served in Chinese and Korean households at the New Year to symbolize wealth and success, coin-shaped rice cakes are delicious, substantial rice "noodles" that make great substrate for a quick stir-fry. My version, which isn't authentic to any particular region but borrows from delicious renditions at Chinese restaurants here, is a combination of hearty shiitake mushrooms, a good dose of leafy greens, and the chew of vegan chicken. Look for the rice cakes and gai lan (Chinese broccoli) in a well-stocked Asian market, and soak the rice cakes first for an hour, if you can—they'll cook more evenly that way. Also, if your chicken's instructions call for it to be cooked directly from frozen, let it sit at room temperature just long enough that it can be cut with a large knife before cooking. Swirl in a spoonful of chili garlic sauce when serving, if you like a little heat.

Meet the Animals

We have a chicken named Gilligan who started her life at a live market in San Francisco's Chinatown. A local teenager visiting the city saw she was for sale, was horrified, and bought her in order to save her. His mother would have none of it, however, so she came to live at Rancho Compasión. She was quite diseased, it turned out, so we raised her inside the house for the first couple of months while treating her. She loved to perch on top of our heads (yes, we put chicken diapers on her!) or our shoulders and would follow the dogs around. We were concerned that she wouldn't be able to adapt to the flock, but when we finally introduced her, she fit right in. I guess she's quite hot, because she became an immediate favorite of a couple of the roosters, who frequently fight for her attention.

¼ cup cold water

2 tablespoons Chinese black vinegar (see Glossary)

1 tablespoon soy sauce

1 tablespoon finely grated fresh ginger

2 teaspoons cornstarch

1 large clove garlic, grated

1 teaspoon toasted sesame oil

4 tablespoons neutral oil, such as sunflower, canola, avocado, or grapeseed

1 pound gai lan (or similar Asian leafy green, such as bok choy), halved crosswise to separate the stems from the leaves, stems sliced diagonally into ¼-inch coins, leaves cut into ½-inch-thick strips

8 ounces fresh shiitake mushrooms, stems removed, cut into ¼-inch slices

10 ounces store-bought unflavored vegan chicken breasts or strips, such as Gardein, Tofurky, or No Evil; or homemade Juicy Chicken (page 210) or Savory Roasted Chicken (page 212) cut into ½-inch strips

1 pound fresh rice cakes (about 4 cups), soaked in cold water to cover for 1 hour, then drained

1¾ cups vegetable broth or water

1 tablespoon chili garlic sauce (optional)

In a small bowl, whisk together the water, black vinegar, soy sauce, ginger, cornstarch, garlic, and sesame oil to blend and set aside.

In a wok or a large nonstick skillet, heat 2 tablespoons of the neutral oil over high heat until it shimmers. Add the gai lan stems and cook for 1 minute, stirring frequently, then add the mushrooms and cook until touched with brown and wilted, about 3 more minutes. Transfer the vegetables to a large bowl and set aside. Add the remaining 2 tablespoons neutral oil to the pan, then spread the chicken pieces across the pan and cook for 2 minutes, undisturbed, until well browned. Stir the chicken and cook for another 2 minutes, stirring just occasionally, then transfer to the bowl with the vegetables.

Add the rice cakes and the broth to the pan and cook, stirring occasionally, until almost all of the liquid is gone, about 5 minutes. Stir the vinegar mixture and add it to the pan, stir to coat, and then stir in the chicken and vegetable mixture and the gai lan leaves. Reduce the heat to low and cook for another minute or so, until the sauce has thickened and the leaves have wilted. If desired, stir in the chili garlic sauce. Serve piping hot.

Char Siu Pork

Serves 4 as an entrée, or 8 as an appetizer

I've enjoyed versions of this at vegan Chinese restaurants and wanted to be able to make my own at home. The Pork Tenderlove works beautifully, absorbing some of this sweetish sauce. Char siu is basically a versatile Chinese version of barbecued pork with the complex flavors of five-spice powder. It can be the main entrée served over rice or bowls of ramen or noodles, or thinly sliced and tossed in a stir-fry. Additionally, it can be served before an Asian-inspired meal as a tasty appetizer or used as a delicious filling for pot stickers, spring rolls, and even sandwiches or pork buns.

¼ cup maple syrup or sugar

3 tablespoons hoisin sauce

2 tablespoons soy sauce or tamari

2 tablespoons or Shaoxing rice wine or Japanese sake

2 teaspoons toasted sesame oil

¾ teaspoon Chinese five-spice powder

½ teaspoon freshly ground white pepper

6 cloves garlic, peeled

2 thin slices red beet for color (optional)

Neutral oil for the pan

1¼ pounds uncooked Pork Tenderlove (page 199; see Note)

4 heaping bowls of cooked rice or ramen noodles

In a blender, combine the maple syrup, hoisin sauce, soy sauce, rice wine, sesame oil, five-spice powder, white pepper, garlic, and beets and blend until smooth. If you don't care about the red color, just omit the beet, finely mince the garlic by hand, and simply mix all of the ingredients in a bowl.

Preheat the oven to 300°F. Lightly oil a 9-inch square baking dish.

Pour the sauce into the prepared baking dish and place the uncooked pork in it. Flip the pork to coat it with the sauce. Cover with aluminum foil and bake for about 1½ hours, flipping the pork every 30 minutes to recoat it in the sauce until it has absorbed most of it.

Slice and serve with rice or noodles.

Note: You can also make this with fully cooked Pork Tenderlove. To do so, preheat the oven to 350°F. Put the pork and char siu sauce in an oiled baking dish and flip the pork to cover it completely with the sauce. Cover with aluminum foil and bake for about 1 hour, flipping the pork every 20 minutes to recoat it in the sauce.

Tantanmen with Eggplant and Beef in Spicy Miso Sauce

Serves 6

This is a spin on that versatile dish dandan men in Chinese, or tantanmen in Japanese, for which there are so many variations that I thought I'd throw in my own. While the original recipe calls for ground pork, the vegan version isn't easily found, so vegan ground beef has been substituted. To make the meat as succulently delicious as possible, I've cooked it with silky eggplant and a spicy miso sauce. This goes on noodles in a bit of broth, then it's all topped off with a spicy sesame sauce mixed with tangy preserved vegetables. All I can say is "Yum."

EGGPLANT AND BEEF

2 tablespoons peanut, sunflower, or canola oil

1 pound eggplant, preferably Japanese, cut into ½-inch cubes

8 ounces vegan ground beef, such as Meatless Farm, Beyond Meat, Hungry Planet, or Lightlife; or homemade Gluten- and Oil-Free Ground Beef Crumbles (page 195) or Homemade "Raw" Ground Beef (page 193)

¼ cup white or chickpea miso

¼ cup mirin (see Glossary)

¼ cup water

1 tablespoon chili garlic sauce

1 tablespoon chopped garlic

1 tablespoon toasted sesame oil

1 teaspoon cornstarch

NOODLES AND BROTH

1 pound fresh eggless ramen or other Asian-style noodles (seriously, just about any noodle will do), or 12 ounces dry ramen or other Asian noodles, or 6 ramen packets

6 cups vegan chicken broth, such as Better Than Bouillon

Start by preparing the eggplant and beef: Heat the peanut oil in a skillet over medium heat, then add the eggplant. Cover the pan to create steam and cook the eggplant faster and with less oil. Cook, stirring occasionally, until the eggplant is tender and somewhat browned, 4 to 6 minutes. Add the beef and continue to cook for 3 or 4 more minutes, until they are thoroughly cooked (if they are precooked-style crumbles, just cook until they are warm). In a bowl or measuring cup, combine the miso, mirin, water, chili garlic sauce, garlic, sesame oil, and cornstarch and whisk well to dissolve the cornstarch. Pour this over the eggplant and meat and cook for another minute or so, until hot and slightly thickened.

While the eggplant is cooking, put a big pot of water on for the noodles. When it comes to a boil, cook the noodles according to package directions until very al dente (still chewy), then drain them in a colander and run under cold water to stop the cooking process. Set aside.

Now get started on the sauce (most likely you can do this as the water for the noodles comes to a boil): Mix the sesame paste, chili oil, soy sauce, sugar, vinegar, and garlic in a medium bowl. If the sesame paste is extremely thick, you can mix it in a blender. Stir in the peppercorns and preserved vegetables.

In the same pot you cooked the noodles, add the broth, sliced shiitakes, and soy sauce. Bring to a simmer, then add the bok choy and cook for about 2 minutes, until tender. Using tongs or a slotted spoon, remove the bok choy to a plate and set aside.

RECIPE CONTINUES ➻

4 ounces sliced fresh shiitake mushrooms (2 cups)

2 tablespoons soy sauce or tamari

1 pound bok choy, cut into quarters lengthwise

4 green onions (white and green parts), thinly sliced

SPICY SESAME SAUCE

½ cup Chinese sesame paste (don't substitute tahini; see Notes)

¼ to ½ cup chili oil or chili paste (start with less—you can always add more!)

¼ cup soy sauce or tamari

3 tablespoons sugar

2 tablespoons Chinese black vinegar (see Glossary) or sherry vinegar

2 tablespoons chopped garlic

1 tablespoon Sichuan peppercorns (optional, see Notes)

½ cup roughly chopped Chinese preserved vegetables (see Notes)

Add the noodles to the broth briefly to reheat. Using tongs, divide the noodles among six bowls and pour ½ cup to 1 cup of broth into each bowl. Top the noodles with the bok choy, eggplant, and beef, then pour ¼ to ⅓ cup of the spicy sesame sauce on top. Finally, sprinkle the sliced green onions on top and serve immediately.

Notes: Chinese sesame paste differs greatly from tahini in that it is made from whole, toasted sesame seeds, while tahini is made from raw, hulled seeds and therefore tastes very different. Do not substitute tahini for this or your sauce will end up with a very different flavor.

Sichuan peppercorns are very aromatic and delicious, but you can omit them if you can't find them.

Chinese preserved vegetables are mustard stems or radishes pickled with salt and chili paste. They can best be described as salty, spicy, and sour, which comes from the lactic acid bacteria that is produced during the fermentation process of pickling. They are available online or in Asian grocery stores either in cans or bags.

Lemongrass Beef Skewer Rice Bowls with Turmeric Nuoc Cham

Serves 4

Don't be fooled by the rather verbose ingredients list; this is a Vietnamese-inspired rice bowl that comes together in the time it takes the rice to cook. Start that first, then whirl a pan full of fragrant sizzling lemongrass, ginger, garlic, and shallots into a bright take on traditional Vietnamese nuoc cham, drizzle it onto the rice and some easy fresh veggies, and top with a flurry of fresh herbs and lemongrass beef skewers. The key here is the lemongrass. In Vietnam, where I've had the pleasure of taking a few cooking classes, chefs pound lemongrass on a cutting board with the handle of a knife or with a big river rock instead of cutting it. Once it's been mashed to a pulp, they quickly mince it and put a rather impressive amount into a wide variety of dishes. (Side note: It's actually quite easy to travel in Vietnam as a vegan. Veganism is on the rise there, but it's also a Buddhist country, so many people are vegan at least twice a month, on the full moon and the new moon. There are a lot of vegan restaurants!) In any case, if you feel like smashing it, use about ¼ cup of the smashed softened insides of the lemongrass.

I load the browned beef onto skewers for a fun presentation, but you certainly can just eat them as is. In the summer, try them over cold cooked rice noodles instead of the rice. For extra credit, you can garnish this with chopped peanuts and the fried green onions from Spunky Pad Thai with Chicken (page 163).

1½ cups plus 1 tablespoon neutral oil, such as sunflower, canola, avocado, or grapeseed

1 large shallot, finely chopped

⅓ cup (¼-inch-thick) lemongrass coins, from the tender insides of 2 or 3 stalks lemongrass

2 tablespoons grated peeled fresh ginger

3 cloves garlic, grated

In a large (10 inches or larger), deep sauté pan or wok, heat 1 tablespoon of the oil over medium heat. Add the shallots and cook, stirring occasionally, until soft and slightly browned, 2 to 3 minutes. Add the lemongrass, ginger, and garlic and cook for another minute or so, stirring constantly. Transfer the mixture to a blender or food processor, add ¼ cup of the water, ¼ cup of the lime juice, the fish sauce, 1 teaspoon of the sugar, the salt, turmeric, and sriracha. (You can wipe out the pan and set it aside for cooking the beef.) Whirl the sauce until smooth, scraping down the insides of the blender as needed, 2 to 3 minutes total, until all the lemongrass is very finely chopped. Transfer ¼ cup of the lemongrass mixture to a large bowl

RECIPE CONTINUES ➻

½ cup water

¼ cup plus 1 tablespoon lime juice (from 3 large limes), plus 1 lime, cut into 8 wedges

2 tablespoons vegan fish sauce (see Glossary)

2 teaspoons sugar, divided

¾ teaspoon kosher salt, plus more to taste

½ teaspoon ground turmeric

1 teaspoon to 1 tablespoon sriracha sauce (or other chili garlic sauce), to taste

1 red Thai chile, thinly sliced (optional)

16 to 18 ounces store-bought "raw" type vegan beef tips or chunks, such as Gardein Home Style Beefless Tips, frozen; or homemade Marinated Tender Fillet of Beef (page 190), either pre-marinated or not

Freshly ground black pepper

1 cup white rice flour

4 to 6 cups cooked jasmine rice, or as desired for serving

1 English cucumber, halved lengthwise, seeds scraped out, sliced into ¼-inch pieces on a diagonal

1 large carrot, peeled and grated

Leaves from 4 sprigs fresh cilantro

Leaves from 4 sprigs fresh mint

Leaves from 4 sprigs fresh Thai basil

2 green onions, white and green parts, thinly sliced

and set aside; transfer the remaining sauce to a measuring cup. To the measuring cup, add the remaining 1 tablespoon lime juice and 1 teaspoon sugar, the sliced chile, and the remaining ¼ cup water, stir to blend, and set aside.

Heat the skillet over medium-high heat. Add the remaining 1½ cups oil and let it come to 375°F. Meanwhile, add the beef to the bowl with the lemongrass mixture, tossing to coat each piece of beef thoroughly in the yellow sauce (gloves work great here), and season with salt and pepper. Put the rice flour in a small bowl, then, working with a few at a time, roll each piece of the meat in the flour, making sure it's coated on all sides. Transfer it to a plate and repeat with the remaining pieces of meat and rice flour.

When the oil is hot, carefully add the meat to the oil, shaking off any excess flour before you do so. (The pan will be crowded, but in this case, that's okay.) Cook for 5 minutes, then turn and cook for another 3 minutes, or until all the pieces are crisp and browned. Using a slotted spoon, transfer the meat to a paper towel–lined plate. Squeeze 4 of the lime wedges over the meat. Skewer the meat for serving, evenly dividing and threading the pieces among eight short (6-inch) skewers.

Heap 1 to 1½ cups of rice into each of four wide, shallow bowls. Pile some of the cucumber and carrot next to the rice, then tear a sprig's worth of cilantro, mint, and basil leaves over each bowl. Add 2 skewers of meat to each bowl, garnish with the green onions and the 4 remaining lime wedges, and serve immediately, with the sauce in small bowls for each person to add to taste.

Variation

Air-Fried Lemongrass Beef: If you would like to avoid deep-frying and have an air fryer, the beef can be cooked there after coating it in the rice flour. Air-fry for about 10 minutes at the highest setting to get it nice and crispy.

Spunky Pad Thai with Chicken

Serves 4

So, time for a vegan confession. A couple of decades (or more) ago, before Thai food was ubiquitous, I remember frequenting a rare, hole-in-the wall Thai restaurant and chowing down on pad Thai (without the eggs). I wasn't aware (nor were my vegan friends) that Thai food typically gets its deep, umami-rich flavor from fermented fish sauce. When we found out, we wondered momentarily if we were still vegan. In any case, on our next visit, we requested that they leave the fish sauce out. Suddenly, the pad Thai, while still tasty, was a bit lackluster.

You won't find this version here lackluster: It's a super-bright twist on the classic noodle dish—made with seared vegan chicken, turmeric tofu in place of the eggs, a burst of ginger, and crunchy fried shallots on top, it's a nod to some of the best pad Thais I had before I knew about fish sauce.

Luckily, today, there are several options for vegan fish sauce (my favorite being 24 Vegan), and if you can't find any, you could make your own from my recipe in *The Homemade Vegan Pantry*. If you use a vegan chicken breast that instructs you to cook it from frozen, take it out of the freezer about 1 hour before you start cooking so it's sliceable when you begin.

NOODLES

6 to 8 cups boiling water

8 ounces thick rice noodles or rice fettuccine (sometimes labeled "for pad Thai")

10 ounces store-bought vegan chicken, breasts or strips, such as Be Leaf, Layonna, Gardein, Tofurky, or No Evil Foods; or homemade Juicy Chicken (page 210) or Savory Roasted Chicken (page 212), cut into ½-inch strips

4 ounces medium-firm tofu

¼ teaspoon ground turmeric

1 cup mung bean sprouts

5 green onions (white and light green parts), thinly sliced

Pour the boiling water into a bowl. Soak the noodles in the water for 4 to 5 minutes, until they begin to soften but are still toothsome. (Do not boil—simply soaking helps prevent the noodles from getting mushy later. They will be very al dente, which is fine—the noodles will soften when cooked at the end.) Drain and set aside.

Meanwhile, make the sauce: In a small bowl, stir together the fish sauce with the water, lime juice, ginger, sugar, soy sauce, sriracha, and garlic until the sugar has dissolved. Set aside.

Fry the shallots for the topping: In a small saucepan, combine the shallots and oil and bring to a simmer over medium-high heat. Cook, stirring occasionally, until the shallots are crisp and browned, 6 to 8 minutes. Using a slotted spoon, transfer the shallots to a paper towel–lined plate to drain and set aside, reserving the oil.

RECIPE CONTINUES ➤➤

½ cup roughly chopped salted roasted peanuts

¼ cup roughly chopped fresh cilantro

SAUCE

2 tablespoons vegan fish sauce (see Glossary)

½ cup water

2 tablespoons lime juice

1 tablespoon grated peeled fresh ginger

2 teaspoons sugar

2 teaspoons soy sauce or tamari

2 teaspoons sriracha sauce (or other chili garlic sauce), plus more for serving

1 clove garlic, grated

TOPPINGS

1 large shallot, natural sections separated, each sliced into ⅛-inch rings

½ cup neutral oil, such as sunflower, canola, avocado, or grapeseed

1 lime, cut into wedges

Heat a wok or large nonstick skillet over medium-high heat. Add 2 tablespoons of the reserved shallot oil, then add the chicken and cook for about 3 minutes, undisturbed, until well browned. Stir and cook for another 2 minutes, stirring frequently to brown all sides, then transfer to a large bowl and set aside.

In a small bowl, use a fork to mash the tofu with the turmeric. Add another 1 tablespoon of the reserved shallot oil to the skillet, then add the tofu mixture and cook for 1 minute, stirring frequently. Add the bean sprouts, stir for just another moment to soften the sprouts, and pile the whole mixture into the large bowl on top of the chicken.

Add the noodles and sauce to the pan and cook, tossing the noodles with tongs, until each noodle is coated in sauce and the liquid has almost disappeared. Add the chicken mixture, green onions, half of the peanuts, and half of the cilantro to the pan and toss until blended. Serve hot, topped with the fried shallots and the remaining peanuts and cilantro. Serve with lime wedges and extra sriracha for those who like it extra spicy.

Beginner's Indian Butter Chicken

Serves 4

I can't say that I'm a master of Indian cuisine, but if you're like me and feeling a bit of trepidation about jumping in, this butter chicken is the perfect place to start. Slightly spicy but widely appealing, it gets its creaminess from both coconut milk and vegan butter. I like making it with mostly pantry staples and root vegetables, which means it's a good candidate for the end of a busy week—especially if you keep vegan chicken in the freezer. You can gussy it up with some fresh herbs (say, cilantro) if you're so inclined, but I like it for what it is: a comforting, flavorful way to end a hectic week. Serve it with plenty of basmati rice, white or brown—your pick.

1 tablespoon coconut oil

1 yellow onion, chopped

3 cloves garlic, finely chopped

1 tablespoon chopped peeled fresh ginger

1 teaspoon ground cumin

1 teaspoon ground coriander

½ teaspoon ground turmeric

½ teaspoon ground cardamom

½ teaspoon ground cinnamon

½ teaspoon red pepper flakes

1 cup vegetable broth

1 (14-ounce) can full-fat coconut milk

1 (14-ounce) can tomato sauce

2 russet potatoes (about 1¼ pounds), peeled and cut into 1-inch chunks

2 large carrots, cut into ¾-inch rounds

Kosher salt and freshly ground black pepper

10 ounces store-bought vegan chicken, such as Gardein, Tofurky, No Evil, or Be Leaf; or homemade Juicy Chicken (page 210) or Savory Roasted Chicken (page 212), cut into 1-inch pieces

4 tablespoons vegan butter, such as Miyoko's

Cooked long-grain rice for serving

Heat a large, high-sided skillet over medium heat. And the oil and the onions and cook, stirring occasionally, until the onions are beginning to soften, about 3 minutes. Add the garlic and ginger and cook for another minute or so, stirring continuously. Add the cumin, coriander, turmeric, cardamom, cinnamon, and red pepper flakes and cook for another 30 seconds or so, until the spices coat the onions and the bottom and sides of the pan. Add the vegetable broth, scraping up any browned bits off the bottom of the pan as it bubbles away, then stir in the coconut milk and tomato sauce and add the potatoes and carrots. Season with salt and pepper. Bring to a simmer, then reduce the heat to the lowest setting, cover, and cook for 25 to 30 minutes, until the potatoes and carrots are tender. Stir in the chicken and cook, covered, for another 5 minutes. Remove from the heat, season with salt and pepper as needed, crumble the butter over the pan, and stir until the butter has melted. Serve over rice.

Persian Eggplant Stuffed with Spiced Beef and Walnuts

Serves 6

I once had a little lamb who followed me around wherever I went. This little lamb, named Cinnamon, is no longer small, and no longer follows me around—she'd much rather hang out with her sheep friends, that darn teenager. She's a spicy young lady now, and *no way* would I ever consider eating her (or her friends), but I've taken inspiration from her and Persian cuisine to create a spice-filled stuffed eggplant dish that has her name all over it. While the traditional Persian dish is made with lamb, I've substituted vegan ground beef, which is more readily available. To whom do I dedicate this flavorful dish? To Cinnamon, of course!

3 medium globe eggplants, cut in half lengthwise

2 tablespoons olive oil, plus more for brushing the eggplant

1 cup finely chopped walnuts (chopped by hand or pulsed briefly in a food processor)

1 large yellow or white onion, diced

1 red bell pepper, diced

6 cloves garlic, minced

8 ounces store-bought "raw" type vegan ground beef, such as Beyond Meat, Hungry Planet, Sweet Earth, Meatless Farm, or Lightlife; or Homemade "Raw" Ground Beef (page 193)

1 tablespoon soy sauce, tamari, or Bragg Liquid Aminos (see Glossary)

2 teaspoons hot smoked paprika

1½ teaspoons ground cumin

1 teaspoon ground allspice

1 teaspoon ground ginger, or 1 tablespoon grated fresh ginger

½ teaspoon ground cinnamon

Freshly ground black pepper

Preheat the oven to 350°F.

Using a sharp knife, cut crosshatch marks into the top of the cut side of the eggplants. Place the eggplant halves on a sheet pan, cut side up, and brush lightly with olive oil (about a tablespoon—it's easiest if you just dip your fingers and rub the eggplant). Bake for about 30 minutes, until soft.

While you are baking the eggplant, toast ⅔ cup of the walnuts in the oven (set aside the remaining ⅓ cup for topping the eggplant). Place them on a small baking pan and bake for about 8 minutes, until very lightly browned.

Remove the eggplant from the oven and allow to cool briefly (you can stick them in the fridge or freezer for a few minutes if you want, or even do this the day before finishing the dish). After they are cool enough to handle, scrape out the inside of the eggplant halves, being careful to leave the skin intact. Chop the scraped eggplant meat and set aside.

Meanwhile, heat 2 tablespoons olive oil in a skillet, add the onion, bell pepper, and garlic and sauté until tender, about 5 minutes. Add the beef, chopped eggplant, soy sauce, smoked paprika, cumin, allspice, ginger, and cinnamon. Cook for 4 to 5 minutes, until the meat no longer appears raw—it doesn't need to be fully cooked, as it will continue to cook in the oven. Stir in the toasted walnuts, mix well, and season with black pepper.

Stuff the eggplant halves with this mixture and top with the remaining ⅓ cup walnuts. Bake for about 30 minutes, until beautifully browned.

Turkish Beef and Rice Stuffed Squash

Serves 8

Stuffed squash dishes are all over the Middle East, but this one, loosely based on Turkey's etli kabak dolmasi, is accented with fresh mint and cinnamon. It makes for a beautiful presentation that is light, fragrant, and delicious.

8 medium zucchini, preferably nice fat ones

1 pound ripe fresh tomatoes, or 1 (15-ounce) can diced tomatoes

1 yellow or white onion

6 cloves garlic, minced

2 tablespoons olive oil

Sea salt

½ cup medium or short-grain white rice, soaked in water for 10 minutes

6 ounces store-bought "raw" type vegan ground beef, such as Beyond Meat, Meatless Farm, Lightlife, or Sweet Earth; or Homemade "Raw" Ground Beef (page 193)

¼ cup minced fresh parsley

2 tablespoons chopped fresh mint

2 tablespoons tomato paste

¼ teaspoon ground cinnamon

Freshly ground black pepper

1 small red bell pepper

4 ounces Homemade Paneer (page 233), cut into 1-inch squares

Take a knife and lightly scrape off most of the surface of the zucchini, exposing the lighter inside. Cut the zucchini in half, not lengthwise but widthwise in two pieces. Using a grapefruit knife, hollow out the insides of the zucchini from the cut side. Start with a small scoop, then expand out and deeper in, leaving a ¼ to ⅓-inch-thick shell. It's actually easier than it sounds and goes rather fast. Put the scooped-out insides into a deep pan or pot.

Chop the tomatoes (if using fresh) and put about two-thirds of them in the pot along with the insides of the zucchini. Slice half of the onion and throw that into the pot as well. Add about half of the garlic, the olive oil, and a good pinch of salt.

Make the filling: Finely dice the remaining onion half and put it in a bowl. Drain the rice that has been soaking and add it to the bowl, along with the beef, parsley, mint, tomato paste, the remaining garlic and tomatoes, and the cinnamon. Mix well and season with salt and black pepper.

Now stuff the rice-beef filling into the cavities of the zucchini. Cut the red bell pepper into 16 pieces that are roughly the same size as the opening of the zucchini and insert as a top to enclose it. Set the zucchini in the pot so that the open end is angled upward. The zucchini and tomatoes in the pot will help them to stand up a bit. This is important because the pot will be filled with liquid once you put it on the stovetop, and you don't want the liquid to run into the filling.

Put the pan or pot on the stove, cover it, and turn the heat to high. When it comes to a boil, turn down the heat and simmer for 45 minutes, then top each zucchini opening with a square of paneer. Put the lid back on and simmer for an additional 15 minutes, until the liquid is reduced and very flavorful, the zucchini is tender, and the rice is fully cooked. Serve with the sauce in the pot.

Variation

Yogurt-Topped Squash: Skip the paneer and simply serve the squash with a dollop of plain vegan yogurt.

Quickest Creamy Chicken Adobo

Serves 4

Filipino chicken adobo is a classic braised chicken dish. In its original form, chicken browns in a pan, then braises in a heady mixture of rice vinegar, soy sauce, and coconut milk—not exactly a weeknight dinner if you're in a rush. This vegan version is super convenient—in fact, if you substitute frozen veggies for the garnishes, you could make it entirely with what you stock ahead in the pantry or freezer—but still intensely flavorful. Try serving it with steamed broccoli or green beans, or braise a few handfuls of chopped kale right in the sauce with the chicken at the end. Although I've never had the "real thing," our Filipino chef at Miyoko's, Syl, says that it tastes very much like what she grew up on. Serve the chicken over rice in wide, shallow bowls, with a shower of cilantro and green onions.

1 (14-ounce) can full-fat coconut milk

⅓ cup rice vinegar

⅓ cup soy sauce or tamari

1 clove garlic, peeled and smashed

3 dried bay leaves

¾ teaspoon black peppercorns, roughly crushed in a mortar and pestle

10 ounces store-bought vegan chicken breasts, such as Gardein; or homemade Juicy Chicken (page 210) or Savory Roasted Chicken (page 212)

4 cups cooked jasmine or basmati rice

2 tablespoons chopped fresh cilantro

2 green onions (white and green parts), thinly sliced

In a large skillet, stir together the coconut milk, vinegar, soy sauce, garlic, bay leaves, and crushed peppercorns and bring to a simmer over medium heat. Cook for about 10 minutes, stirring occasionally, until the liquid has reduced by about half.

Meanwhile, cook the chicken according to package instructions, if necessary. For homemade Juicy Chicken, simply slide it into the adobo and cook for another 2 minutes to warm it through, turning once or twice during cooking. Serve with rice and top the whole thing with cilantro and green onions.

Moussaka

Serves 8 to 10

On my first trip to Greece in 1978, I was intrigued by a dish called moussaka, which was on restaurant menus everywhere. Being a vegetarian, I never ate it (instead, I lived off of spanakopita and tyropita), although I made sure someone explained to me what it was made of. Eggplant covered in thick layers of cinnamon-laced beefy ragu topped with béchamel sauce makes for a transformative experience. A layer of potatoes isn't a must, but I think it makes it even better. What to serve with it? A real Greek salad made with of chopped tomatoes, red onions, olives, and vegan feta—no lettuce, as that is not traditional.

2 pounds globe, Italian, or Japanese eggplant, sliced ½ inch thick

Sea salt

1½ pounds Yukon Gold potatoes

MEAT SAUCE

About 5 tablespoons olive oil

1 yellow or white onion, diced

1 tablespoon minced garlic, or to taste

1 pound store-bought vegan ground beef, such as Beyond Meat, Lightlife, Hungry Planet; or Plant Ranch Carne Asada; or Homemade "Raw" Ground Beef (page 193)

2 tablespoons soy sauce, tamari, or Bragg Liquid Aminos (see Glossary)

28 ounces very ripe fresh tomatoes, chopped, or 1 (28-ounce) can diced tomatoes

½ cup red wine

4 tablespoons tomato paste

2 teaspoons dried oregano

1 teaspoon hot smoked paprika

1 teaspoon sugar

½ teaspoon ground cinnamon, or 1 cinnamon stick

2 bay leaves

Freshly ground black pepper

Sprinkle the eggplant with salt and put it in a colander in the sink to allow it to exude its bitter juice. If you are using Italian or Japanese eggplant, you can simply slice them and skip this salting step.

Put the potatoes in a pot of water with a pinch of salt and bring to a boil. Turn the heat down to a simmer and cook until the potatoes are fork-tender, about 30 minutes. Remove from the water and allow them to cool, then peel the skin and slice them about ¼ inch thick.

Meanwhile, get started on the meat sauce: Heat 3 tablespoons of the olive oil in a large heavy-bottom pan. Add the onion and garlic and sauté until tender, about 5 minutes. Crumble the ground beef into the pan and cook until browned, about 3 minutes; drizzle in the soy sauce and stir to incorporate. Add the tomatoes, red wine, tomato paste, oregano, smoked paprika, sugar, cinnamon, and bay leaves. Bring to a simmer and cook for about 30 minutes, until the mixture is very thick and delicious looking. Season with salt and pepper.

EXTRA-THICK BÉCHAMEL SAUCE

4 cups water

1½ cups raw cashews

⅓ cup white wine

¼ cup cornstarch

1 tablespoon nutritional yeast
(see Glossary)

½ teaspoon sea salt

½ cup store-bought grated vegan
Parmesan cheese, such as Violife; or
cheddar cheese, such as Miyoko's
or Violife; or Homemade Hard Parmesan
(page 236); or Quickie Nut Parm
(page 177)

Freshly ground black pepper

While the sauce is cooking, prepare the extra-thick béchamel sauce:
Combine the water, cashews, wine, cornstarch, nutritional yeast, and salt
in a blender and blend until smooth and creamy. Pour into a saucepan and
cook over medium heat, stirring with a wooden spoon or whisk, until it
becomes very thick, which will happen when it comes to a simmer, about
3 minutes. Stir in the cheese and pepper.

Now cook the eggplant slices. Heat a large skillet over high heat and
pour in the remaining 2 tablespoons olive oil. Add as many eggplant
slices as will fit in a single layer and sear both sides until browned, about
2 minutes. Keep the heat relatively high, as you want to sear the outsides
without allowing the slices to get mushy; they will continue to cook in
the oven. Remove the slices from the pan and set aside. Repeat with the
remaining eggplant, adding 1 or 2 tablespoons of olive oil to the pan each
time until all of the eggplant has been cooked.

Preheat the oven to 375°F.

Now you are ready to assemble the moussaka. In a 9 by 13-inch baking
dish, place a layer of the eggplant closely together, using about half of the
total eggplant. Pour half of the sauce over the first layer of eggplant slices
and top with the remaining eggplant. Pour the remaining sauce over this
layer, then top with the potato slices. Spread the cashew béchamel sauce
over the eggplant. Bake for about 30 minutes, until the top is browned.
Allow the moussaka to cool for about 15 minutes before slicing and serving.

Pasta e Fagioli with Pancetta

Serves 4

In its most basic form, Italian pasta e fagioli is a vegetable-studded, tomato-based stew with pasta and beans (hence the name). Its magic comes from its infinite flexibility: Meat-eaters often add pancetta or guanciale (cured pork jowl), gardeners use it as a repository for a never-ending zucchini harvest, and I adore its ability to absorb chopped leftover anything. This one has an unctuous, meaty flavor that comes from chopped dried porcini mushrooms. They don't really register here as mushrooms, but rather as a rich, meaty background flavor—perfect for someone who might need a gateway meal to veganism. Use homemade pancetta or bacon if you like a bit of chew and a smokier flavor, or use store-bought vegan Italian sausage if you're pressed for time but still want a super-satisfying stew. And above all, treat this as a template—add what appeals to you! But always serve with a ragged chunk of really great bread.

1 ounce dried porcini mushrooms

1 cup hot water

1 tablespoon extra-virgin olive oil

1 yellow or white onion, finely chopped

2 carrots, sliced into ¼-inch coins

2 stalks celery, cut into ¼-inch
half moons

2 cloves garlic, finely chopped

Kosher salt and freshly ground
black pepper

2 tablespoons tomato paste

2 teaspoons chopped fresh oregano

4 cups vegetable broth

1 pound very ripe fresh tomatoes, diced,
or 1 (15-ounce) can crushed tomatoes

1 small bunch kale or other leafy greens
(about 4 ounces), stems removed,
roughly chopped

2 (15-ounce) cans cannellini beans,
rinsed and drained

½ cup small pasta, such as orzo, ditalini,
or macaroni

1 tablespoon sherry vinegar, plus more
to taste

12 ounces homemade Pancetta
(page 208) or King Trumpet Mushroom
Bacon (page 205); or 2 store-bought
vegan Italian sausages (7 ounces), such
as Beyond Meat, cooked according to
the recipe or package instructions, then
cut into bite-size pieces

Store-bought grated vegan Parmesan
cheese, such as Violife; or Homemade
Hard Parmesan (page 236) or Quickie
Nut Parm (page 177) for serving

Good extra-virgin olive oil for serving

In a small bowl, soak the porcini mushrooms in the hot water for
30 minutes.

Heat a large, heavy soup pot over medium heat. Add the olive oil, then
the onion and cook, stirring occasionally, for 5 minutes, or until the onion
begins to soften. Add the carrots, celery, and garlic, season with salt and
pepper, and cook for another 5 minutes, stirring occasionally. Stir in the
tomato paste and oregano and cook another 2 minutes or so, until the
mixture begins to darken and stick to the pan. Remove the mushrooms
from the water and chop them, reserving the liquid. Add the chopped
mushrooms to the pot along with the vegetable broth, diced or crushed
tomatoes, and kale. Blend or mash 1 can's worth of the beans together
with the reserved porcini soaking water, then add that to the pan. Bring
the soup to a simmer, cover, lower the heat, and cook for 10 minutes,
stirring occasionally. Add the pasta and the remaining whole beans and
cook, stirring occasionally, until the pasta is tender, another 12 minutes or
so. Stir in the vinegar, then season with additional salt and pepper. Stir in
the meat and serve piping hot, topped with grated cheese and a swirl of
good olive oil.

Moon Carbonara

Serves 4 to 6

On a visit to Ortigia, Sicily a few years ago, I had the pleasure of dining at a beautiful vegan restaurant and art gallery called Moon, where our group feasted on local dishes while listening to a passionate Italian singer-songwriter. One of the dishes was a classic carbonara, a creamy pasta dish made with eggs and ham, something that had seemed almost elusive in my vegan dining experience thus far. Provided with a very loose description of how they made it, I've attempted to re-create it here. If you excel at chopping, the whole dish can be made in the time it takes to boil the water and cook the pasta, making it fantastic even for a weeknight. For credibility, use kala namak, aka black salt—its sulfurous flavor will lend an eggy flavor.

Kosher salt

3 tablespoons olive oil

1 yellow or white onion, diced

4 cloves garlic, sliced or minced

8 to 10 ounces Pancetta (preferred; page 208), diced, or store-bought smoked tofu

1 pound linguine

2 cups unsweetened plain or "original" flavor oat or soy milk

⅔ cup chickpea flour

Large pinch of ground turmeric

½ teaspoon black salt (kala namak; see Glossary) or sea salt

½ cup grated store-bought vegan Parmesan, such as Violife or Follow Your Heart; or Homemade Hard Parmesan (page 236) or Quickie Nut Parm (recipe follows), plus more for topping

½ cup chopped fresh parsley

Start by bringing a pot of salted water to a boil for the pasta. While the water is coming to a boil, cook the onion and Pancetta: Heat the olive oil in a sauté pan and add the onions, garlic, and Pancetta and sauté until the onions are tender and the Pancetta is browned, about 7 minutes. Turn off the heat and set aside.

In the pot of boiling salted water, start cooking the linguine. Meanwhile, get the "egg" mixture ready: Put the milk, chickpea flour, and turmeric in a blender and blend briefly until smooth. When the pasta is very al dente— still with a hard middle—drain it, reserving about 1 cup of the pasta cooking water. Pour the pasta into the pan with the onions and pancetta, turn the heat back to medium, and pour in the milk-chickpea "egg" mixture. Stir well; the mixture will begin to thicken and coat the linguine quickly. Add the black salt. If the mixture seems too thick and gummy, add some or all of the additional pasta water. The mixture should be nice and creamy, not gummy. Stir in the cheese and parsley and serve, with additional cheese as desired.

Quickie Nut Parm

Makes about 2½ cups

There are lots of nut Parmesan recipes out there, but the addition of green olives brings a bit more complexity and Parmesan-like flavor to this instant solution for sprinkling on pasta and salads.

1 cup walnuts, almonds, pine nuts, or roasted pumpkin seeds, or a mixture

1 cup nutritional yeast (see Glossary)

½ cup pitted green olives

½ teaspoon sea salt

Put all of the ingredients in a food processor and process until a fine, crumbly texture is achieved. Keep it in a jar in the refrigerator for 6 to 8 weeks.

Sausage and Porcini Ragu over Polenta
(Ragù de Salsiccia e Porcini)

Serves 6

Variations of a hearty ragu made from wild mushrooms and sausage can be found all over Italy. While it might sound like food for nobility, it was likely, in fact, the peasant's way of creating a delicious repast by foraging for mushrooms in the woods (still a favorite pastime for Italians) and throwing in a flavorful sausage or two, which, as we know, were made from the leftover cuts of animals. But we needn't linger on the latter, less-than-savory memories of yore: Here, vegan sausages marry dried porcini mushrooms in a rich tomato-based ragu, served over creamy, soft polenta for a perfect Italian repast fit for a candlelight dinner by the fireplace. The polenta cooks itself in the oven while you pay attention to the ragu on the stovetop, so you needn't worry about the constant stirring required for most polenta recipes. If you like, you can make the polenta ahead of time (even the day before), pour it into a baking dish, and let it set up to get firm on the counter or fridge. When you're ready to serve, cut and pan-fry it until golden brown on both sides.

If your liking is more for pasta, go ahead and serve it with pasta instead, but don't even think of anything delicate like angel hair—this is deserving of something bigger, bolder, and chewier, such as a fat pappardelle or rigatoni.

POLENTA

6 cups water

1 teaspoon sea salt

1¼ cups dry polenta (coarse cornmeal)

2 tablespoons nutritional yeast
(see Glossary)

5 cloves garlic, minced

1 tablespoon olive oil

RAGU

1 ounce dried porcini mushrooms

1 cup hot water

3 tablespoons olive oil

4 large "raw" type vegan Italian
sausages, such as Beyond Meat or
Lightlife

1 yellow onion, diced

1 fennel bulb, cored, cut in half, and
thinly sliced (reserve the fronds—the
feathery part of the fennel)

Sea salt

1¾ pounds very ripe fresh tomatoes,
chopped, or 1 (28-ounce) can diced
San Marzano tomatoes

¼ cup red wine

6 cloves garlic, minced

2 tablespoons tomato paste

2 sprigs fresh rosemary

½ teaspoon red pepper flakes

¼ cup reserved finely chopped
fennel fronds for garnish

Start by making the polenta: Preheat the oven to 375°F.

Bring the water to a boil in a large ovenproof pot, such as a Dutch oven, then add the salt. Using a wire whisk, whisk the polenta into the pot in a steady stream, whisking all the while (don't just dump it all in or it could clump up). Add the nutritional yeast, garlic, and olive oil and whisk well. Cover the pot and put it in the oven to finish cooking on its own for about 45 minutes, until thick, creamy, and smooth.

After you've put the polenta into the oven, start the ragu: Put the porcini in a small bowl and pour the hot water over, allowing them to soak while you prepare the sauce. In a heavy-bottom pan, heat the olive oil over medium heat, then add the sausages and cook for 3 or 4 minutes, until browned. The sausages will ooze a bit of fat and juice, adding flavor to the other ingredients that will be cooked in the same skillet. Remove the sausages and set aside for later.

Add the onion and fennel to the pan, sprinkle with a pinch of salt, and sauté until tender, about 4 minutes. Add the tomatoes, wine, and garlic and simmer for 15 to 20 minutes, until it has reduced and begins to resemble tomato sauce. Add the tomato paste, rosemary, and red pepper flakes. Remove the porcini from the water and add them to the sauce along with the soaking liquid, being careful not to add the last teaspoon or so, as it can contain sediment (alternatively, you can strain it through cheesecloth or a coffee filter). Finally, slice the sausages about ⅓ inch thick and add them to the sauce. Continue to simmer for about 5 minutes to allow all of the flavors to meld.

Pile the polenta into individual bowls and spoon a hefty serving of the ragu over it. Garnish with the fennel fronds.

Variations

Ragu over Polenta Squares: If you prefer firm polenta, pour the hot polenta into a well-oiled (use olive oil) dish so that it is about 1 inch thick. Let it cool at room temperature for 1 hour, then refrigerate until firm. Cut it into squares or triangles as desired and pan-fry in olive oil until crispy and browned on both sides. Serve with the ragu.

Stovetop Polenta: If you prefer, you can cook the polenta on the stovetop. Follow the instructions above, but instead of putting it in the oven, turn the heat down to low after all of the ingredients have been added and keep stirring every couple of minutes until it's thick and creamy, 30 to 40 minutes.

Paella with Scallops, Sausage, and Chicken

Serves 6 to 8

Ideally, you will have a large paella pan, an open fire pit on which to place it, and a Spanish sunset over golden hills when you make this. But even in a cramped Chicago apartment, you can still transport your family and friends to a romantic setting with this unctuous dish with layers of flavor. Paella, the national dish of Spain, is traditionally made in a wide, shallow, thin pan that heats quickly and cooks the rice evenly. Use your largest skillet or even a cast-iron pan, and I guarantee, no one will be the wiser.

If you have leftover Quick Buttery Scallops, you can skip the step of prepping and cooking the king trumpet mushrooms and just use them instead.

1 ounce dried porcini mushrooms

2 cups hot water

6 tablespoons olive oil

8 ounces king trumpet mushrooms, cut into ½-inch discs, or 8 ounces of Quick Buttery Scallops (page 230)

1 tablespoon vegan fish sauce (see Glossary; skip if using leftover Quick Buttery Scallops)

9 ounces vegan Italian sausage, such as Gardein, Field Roast, Tofurky, or Beyond Meat, sliced ½-inch thick

9 ounces store-bought vegan chicken breast or drumsticks, such as Layonna or Be Leaf, sliced ½ inch thick; or vegan chicken strips or chunks or such as Gardein, Plant Ranch Pollo Asada, Tofurky, Better Chew, or No Evil Foods; or homemade Juicy Chicken (page 210) or Savory Roasted Chicken (page 212), sliced ½ inch thick

2 yellow or white onions, diced

1 red, yellow, or orange bell pepper, diced

5 cloves garlic, minced

½ cup minced fresh parsley

Sea salt

In a small bowl, soak the porcini mushrooms in the hot water for about 20 minutes. Meanwhile, heat 2 tablespoons of the olive oil in a large skillet over medium heat and add the king trumpet mushrooms. Let them brown on one side, about 3 minutes, then flip them over and cook for about 3 minutes more. When both sides are browned, splash the fish sauce over them, then remove and set aside (skip this step if you have Quick Buttery Scallops on hand). In the same pan, heat another 2 tablespoons of the olive oil and add the sausage and chicken, cooking until lightly browned over medium heat, about 4 minutes. Add these to the scallops and set aside.

Heat the remaining 2 tablespoons olive oil in the pan and add the onions, bell peppers, garlic, and parsley to make sofrito. Sprinkle with a dash of salt and sauté until the vegetables are tender, about 4 minutes.

2 cups short-grain white rice, such as arborio

2 large pinches of saffron

1½ cups vegetable stock

1¾ pounds ripe, fresh tomatoes, diced, or 1 (28-ounce) can diced tomatoes

½ cup red wine

2 teaspoons dried basil

Freshly ground black pepper

Add the rice and saffron and cook, stirring for 2 minutes. Add the scallops, sausage, chicken, porcini mushrooms with their soaking liquid, vegetable stock, tomatoes, wine, basil, and a dash or two of black pepper and give it a quick stir. Cover well, turn the heat low, and cook until the rice is tender, about 15 minutes.

Sicilian Chicken and Cauliflower in Red Wine with Olives and Capers

Serves 4 to 6

This was a dish I had in Sicily senza (without) the chicken. Adding plant-based chicken to it makes it a complete entrée that needs just a salad and rice or a bit of pasta to complete it. The chef who created it and taught us how to make it kept repeating that there was no water used to braise the cauliflower. It's all red wine, baby, giving a lovely purple hue to everything. The smoked cheese adds roundness and fullness of flavor. Smoked mozzarella is traditional, but other types of smoked cheese work as well (just make sure the cheese is truly smoked and doesn't just contain smoke flavor, as that can affect the overall outcome of the dish). If you like a little heat, a bit of peperoncino (red pepper flakes) would be fine to add. Serve with pasta or rice—I prefer a fluffy, long-grain rice for this, or just a big chunk of crusty bread to mop up the sauce.

2 tablespoons olive oil

1 red onion, diced

3 cloves garlic, minced

1 head cauliflower, cut into florets

12 ounces store-bought vegan chicken strips or large chunks (not "chopped"), such as Gardein, Tofurky, or Better Chew (personal favorite); or homemade Juicy Chicken (page 210) or Savory Roasted Chicken (page 212)

1½ cups red wine

⅔ cup kalamata olives, pitted and cut in half

⅓ cup capers

Pinch of red pepper flakes (optional)

6 ounces vegan smoked mozzarella or other smoked vegan cheese, such as Miyoko's, grated

½ cup pine nuts, toasted (see Note, page 40)

Sea salt

Minced parsley for garnishing (optional)

In a deep heavy-bottom pan or pot with a tight-fitting cover, heat the olive oil on medium-low. Add the onions and garlic and sauté until tender, about 4 minutes (you can use a cover to expedite). Add the cauliflower, chicken, wine, olives, capers, and red pepper flakes, cover, and simmer for 12 to 15 minutes, until the cauliflower is very tender. Stir the contents once or twice to ensure even coating of the cauliflower and render it all a lovely pink hue. In the end, there should be a bit of red juice remaining, but the contents shouldn't be swimming in wine. Add the cheese and pine nuts and stir to melt the cheese. Season with salt as desired and garnish with parsley.

Albondigas

Serves 4 to 6

Albondigas are the Mexican grandmother's version of the ultimate comfort food. They're meatballs typically based on a beef mixture and are often made with rice and herbs and usually quite light in texture. Colloquially, many people think of albondigas not as the meatballs themselves, which I believe is technically correct, but as the brothy, vegetable-studded soup they make famous, which goes by the same name. This is my vegan version of both—meatballs lightened with cooked brown rice and freshened up with chopped herbs, in a savory broth that's satisfying but not too weighty. Mint isn't always traditional here, but I find it gives the soup brightness in the winter and a refreshing boost in the summer, so in it goes, all year 'round. If you prefer, you can use cilantro instead.

SOUP

2 tablespoons extra-virgin olive oil

1 small yellow onion, chopped

2 carrots, halved lengthwise and cut crosswise into ½-inch half moons

2 stalks celery, halved lengthwise if especially fat, cut into ½-inch pieces

2 large cloves garlic, finely chopped

1 tablespoon finely chopped fresh oregano

2 tablespoons tomato paste

¾ teaspoon ground cumin

¼ teaspoon ground coriander

Kosher salt and freshly ground black pepper

8 cups vegetable broth

2 vine-ripe tomatoes, chopped

1 (12-ounce) russet potato, peeled and cut into ¾-inch pieces

¼ cup chopped fresh mint, plus more for serving

Make the soup: Heat a large soup pot or Dutch oven over medium heat. Add the oil and onion and cook, stirring occasionally, until the onion begins to soften, about 3 minutes. Add the carrots, celery, and garlic and cook for another 2 minutes, stirring frequently. Stir in the oregano, tomato paste, cumin, and coriander, season with salt and pepper, and stir until all the vegetables are well coated, another minute or so. Add the broth, tomatoes, and potato and bring to a boil. Reduce the heat to low and simmer for 15 minutes until the flavors have melded and the soup is flavorful.

Meanwhile, make the meatballs: In a medium bowl, stir together the rice, oregano, mint, garlic, salt, cumin, coriander, and black pepper to blend. Add the beef and mix until the rice is thoroughly blended into the meat and the mixture is uniform. (I find hands work best here.) Form the mixture into about two dozen 1-inch meatballs. (If you'd like to make the soup ahead, stop here. Let the soup come to room temperature and refrigerate, covered, for up to 3 days. Cover and refrigerate the meatballs as well. Before serving, bring the soup back up to a simmer and continue.)

MEATBALLS

1 cup cooked brown rice

1 tablespoon finely chopped fresh oregano

1 tablespoon finely chopped fresh mint

2 large cloves garlic, grated

½ teaspoon kosher salt

½ teaspoon ground cumin

¼ teaspoon ground coriander

¼ teaspoon freshly ground black pepper

1 pound "raw" type vegan ground beef, such as Beyond Meat, Hungry Planet, Meatless Farm, Sweet Earth, or Lightlife

Add the mint and meatballs to the soup and simmer gently for 10 minutes, or until the meat is no longer pink in the center, gently turning the meatballs about halfway through. Season the soup with salt and pepper and serve, with extra mint on top.

CHAPTER 6

Just Make It:
The DIY Art of Making Vegan Meat
and Cheese from Plants

When there is such a plethora of new products hitting shelves, why would you want to go to the trouble of making your own meat alternatives? First of all, there is magic in taking grains, legumes, or fungi and turning them into something entirely new. And then there's the opportunity to make a range of products that are less processed, maybe even whole foods–based or gluten-free, with cleaner ingredients. Finally, there's the opportunity to make things that aren't yet readily available, such as vegan lobster! No, they won't be the spitting image of animal flesh (which we likely don't want, anyway), but I guarantee that they are more than adequately delicious.

The chapter kickstarts with creative versions of the more traditional meats made from wheat gluten. However, I've "elevated" them by incorporating mushrooms, legumes, and other grains to create different flavors and textures than what you normally find. From a chewy, succulent steak, to a flaky brisket, to a juicy chicken—it's all here. But the recipes based on seitan are only a handful—the majority of recipes in this chapter are gluten-free and feature unique preparations of mushrooms, legumes, and konjac to create everything from fish to fried chicken. I've even included an instant burger mix that you can make and keep in your pantry for when you need a quick, healthy, but "meaty" meal.

Even though this is a book about plant-based meat, I couldn't possibly not throw in a few cheese recipes. After all, cheese and meat so often go hand in hand. I remember just a few years ago when vegan cheese was the butt of jokes. Now multiple brands occupy major shelf space in grocery stores beyond just natural food stores. Just like alternative milks, which now represent 15 percent of the sales of fluid milk, seriously cutting into the market share of dairy milk, vegan cheeses are on their way to impacting how Americans look at grilled cheese sandwiches and pizza.

While my company, Miyoko's, has played a leadership role in helping grow this vegan cheese revolution, there are so many other exciting brands joining the fold and expanding the category that it is a truly exciting time for cheese lovers all around the world. Today, at any grocer, you won't have trouble finding most of the cheeses for the recipes in the preceding chapters of this book. But as I've discovered on my jaunts around the world visiting artisan vegan cheese makers, making your own cheese is a passion project for many vegans. I hope you enjoy the addition of these new recipes!

These are the recipes that really get me excited because they bring out my inner magician. Perhaps it'll bring out yours, too.

Charbroiled Succulent Steak

Makes 8 (8-ounce) steaks

This is the base for a number of dishes, including Cassoulet (page 119) and Hasselback Steak (page 124). It truly is full of flavor and can be thrown into stir-fries, stroganoff, goulash, or Philly cheesesteak sandwiches. It's also delicious as a traditional stand-alone "steak" accompanied by a baked potato and a salad. The charbroiled flavor is essential, so do cook them outdoors on your grill or on the stovetop on a cast-iron grill.

STEAK

1 cup cooked chickpeas

½ cup red wine

½ cup water or additional red wine

5 tablespoons olive oil, plus more for greasing

⅓ cup tomato paste

6 ounces white or cremini mushrooms (about 3 cups), quartered

4 ounces raw red beet (about ½ large beet), peeled and sliced

8 cloves garlic, peeled

3 tablespoons white or chickpea miso

2 tablespoons soy sauce

1 tablespoon vegan beef base, such as Better Than Bouillon

1½ tablespoons smoked paprika

1½ tablespoons onion powder

½ teaspoon freshly ground black pepper

3½ to 4 cups vital wheat gluten (see Glossary)

RUBBING MARINADE

½ cup red wine

⅓ cup olive oil

⅓ cup coarsely ground black pepper

1 tablespoon minced garlic

2 teaspoons dried thyme

1 teaspoon dried rosemary

½ teaspoon kosher salt

Make the steak: Combine all the ingredients except the wheat gluten in a blender and blend until liquefied. Pour the mixture into a large bowl and mix in the wheat gluten with a wooden spoon. Turn out the mixture onto a clean counter and knead for about 2 minutes until very elastic. Pull and pat it out to a thickness of ½ to ¾ inch, then divide it into 8 pieces, either by tearing it by hand or cutting with a knife.

Prepare a steamer by putting water in the bottom. If you don't have a steamer, you can use a colander in a large pot—just make sure that the colander "hangs" on the rim so the bottom is not submerged in water and that you have a lid to cover it. Tear aluminum foil into pieces that are large enough for each steak and brush oil on each piece, then wrap the pieces very loosely in the foil. Place the steaks in the steamer basket, stacking them as necessary. Put the lid on the steamer.

Steam for about 1 hour. To check for doneness, slice into the middle of one of the steaks to see if it is cooked through—it should no longer be gummy but have a consistent texture throughout.

While the steaks are steaming, prepare the rubbing marinade by mixing all of the ingredients in a bowl. Allow the steaks to cool, then rub the marinade all over on both sides.

Heat an outdoor grill or a stovetop cast-iron grill pan until hot. Sear on both sides until charbroiled marks appear. Serve immediately or refrigerate for up to 1 week. You can also freeze the steaks, wrapped separately in plastic wrap or parchment paper in a tightly sealed container, for up to 6 months (thaw before using).

Marinated Tender Fillet of Beef

Makes about 2½ pounds

Unlike Charbroiled Succulent Steak (page 188), which is firm and chewy, this is a tender, thin fillet that bursts with flavor as it melts in your mouth. You can grill this, stuff it, toss it in a stir-fry, use as a flavorful sandwich filling, or add some whole grain mustard to the marinade to make a lovely glaze to enrobe the fillets for a quick and elegant dinner. It's also perfect for Stovetop Beef or Chicken Parmigiana (page 106) or Lemongrass Beef Skewer Rice Bowls (page 161).

An easy change to the ingredients and process will allow you to make the versatile Homemade "Raw" Ground Beef (page 193).

FILLETS

1 cup dried shiitake mushrooms, soaked in about 3 cups water for 3 to 4 hours, or overnight

6 tablespoons soy sauce, tamari, or Bragg Liquid Aminos (see Glossary)

¼ cup olive oil, plus more for the pan

¼ cup red wine

⅓ cup diced yellow or white onion

6 cloves garlic, peeled

2¼ to 2¾ cups vital wheat gluten (see Glossary)

MARINADE

1 cup red wine

¼ cup soy sauce or tamari

¼ cup mirin (see Glossary)

½ cup shiitake soaking liquid

6 cloves garlic, minced

Hefty pinch of freshly ground black pepper

Make the fillets: Remove the shiitakes from the soaking liquid, reserving ½ cup of the liquid or the fillets and ½ cup for the marinade below. Combine ½ cup of the shiitake soaking liquid, the reconstituted shiitakes, 4 tablespoons of the soy sauce, the olive oil, wine, onion, and garlic in a blender and blend until smooth. Pour into a bowl and mix in the wheat gluten, adding the higher amount for chewier, denser texture. (The amount also depends on how much water your shiitakes have absorbed, so adjust accordingly. It should feel like very pliable Play-Doh that can stretch and be formed but not fall apart or be too tough.) Tear into pieces and pat to form fillets about ⅓ inch thick. Heat some oil in a deep skillet, then cook the fillets over medium heat on both sides until browned, about 3 minutes per side. Pour the remaining shiitake soaking liquid and enough water over the fillets to cover completely. Add the remaining 2 tablespoons soy sauce. Partially cover and simmer for about 30 minutes, until fully cooked and tender but not rubbery.

While you are cooking the fillets, make the marinade: Combine all of the ingredients in a bowl. After the fillets have cooked, remove them from the pan and place in the marinade. Cover and allow to marinate for a minimum of 4 hours or overnight in the refrigerator. They will keep in the marinade, refrigerated, for up to 1 week or they can be frozen in the marinade for several months.

Variations

Wine-Free Fillet of Beef: If you are avoiding wine, you can swap it for a flavorful vegetable broth plus 2 tablespoons balsamic vinegar.

Easy Skillet Fillets with Red Wine and Mustard Sauce: Remove the fillets from the marinade, reserving 1 cup of the marinade. Put a skillet over medium-high heat and get it nice and hot. Add 2 tablespoons olive oil, then add the fillets (as many as will fit in your skillet) and sear them until browned on both sides, about 4 minutes. Mix 2 tablespoons whole grain mustard into the reserved 1 cup red wine marinade and pour over the fillets in the pan. Let simmer and cook down until the marinade forms a glaze that enrobes the steaks, 2 to 3 minutes. Serve with a side of potatoes or rice and some green veggies or a salad.

Not Mrs. Maisel's Brisket but Marvelous Nevertheless

Makes 2 pounds

I don't know if this resembles the brisket that Mrs. Maisel carted around from one New York dive bar to another trying to cajole club owners into giving her husband a shot on the stage for comedy night. In fact, I don't know if it resembles brisket at all, never having had it in my life. But after hearing about the power of brisket on the hit television series *The Marvelous Mrs. Maisel*, I asked non-vegan friends what it was. The fact that I tried to create a vegan version based on a mere description from friends may be as funny as the show itself. However, after eating it, I doubt you'll be laughing. I hope you'll be swooning. Is it as "real" as the "real thing"? Who knows? Life is sometimes like television, and we can always use a bit of imagination. The important thing is that it's deliciously tender, full of umami, and highly versatile. While it holds together when sliced, it'll fall apart into beautiful, sinewy strands like pulled pork when stir-fried, and it makes beautiful fajitas or a filling for enchiladas, stuffed bell peppers, or just about anything. You'll see it featured in recipes throughout the book.

5 ounces quartered white or cremini mushrooms (about 2½ cups)

¾ cup red wine

½ cup water

¼ cup plus 2 tablespoons olive oil

¼ cup soy sauce or tamari

4 cloves garlic, peeled

2 cups vital wheat gluten (see Glossary)

¾ cup unsweetened pea protein powder (see Glossary)

4 cups vegan beef broth, such as Better Than Bouillon

In a blender, combine the mushrooms, ½ cup of the red wine, the water, ¼ cup of the olive oil, the soy sauce, and garlic. Blend until smooth, then pour into a large bowl. In a separate bowl, combine the wheat gluten and pea protein and mix well, then add it to the liquid mixture and mix well by hand. Turn out onto a clean surface and knead for about 3 minutes. You should see it become sinewy and stringy. Divide into 4 pieces and roll them into logs about 6 inches long each. Flatten them so that they are about ½ inch thick and about 3 inches wide. (If you want just one large or two medium briskets, you can make them bigger, but they will take an additional 20 or so minutes to cook.)

Heat the remaining 2 tablespoons olive oil in a large, deep frying pan and cook the raw briskets on both sides until browned, about 2 minutes per side. Pour the broth and the remaining ¼ cup red wine over the brisket, cover with a lid, and simmer over medium heat for 30 to 40 minutes. To check for doneness, slice into the middle of one of the pieces; it should not be gummy and have a consistent texture and color throughout. Allow to cool before handling. It will firm up a bit as it cools. You can make this up to 3 days in advance and store in the fridge or freeze for up to 3 months (thaw before using).

Homemade "Raw" Ground Beef

Makes about 1 pound 6 ounces

Here's a "raw" type of vegan ground round that, if made right, will stick together for a burger or meatloaf or cook up as ground beef, turning from red to brown, for meat sauces, tacos, and so on. I have to say, however, that the timing can be a bit tricky, as it can easily be overcooked, losing its ability to stick together. But all would not be lost, however, because even if you overcook it, it can at least be used as crumbles in dishes where cohesion isn't important. The important thing is to cook it long enough that the gluten starts to be activated but the inside remains nice and pink—if it is mostly brown, it has cooked too long and you won't be able to form meatballs and such.

In terms of flavor, this won't have as strong of a meaty flavor as the commercial types with added natural flavors. It's fairly neutral, which means that you can add whatever seasonings you want—make it Mexican, make it Italian, just go to town.

½ cup water

¼ cup olive or other oil, such as sunflower, canola, avocado, or grapeseed

¼ cup diced red beet

¼ cup Bragg Liquid Aminos (see Glossary)

2 tablespoons vegan beef-flavored base, such as Better Than Bouillon, or 4 vegan beef bouillon cubes

3 ounces cremini mushrooms (about 1½ cups), quartered

3 cloves garlic, peeled

¾ cup oat flour

3 tablespoons ground flaxseed

1¼ cups vital wheat gluten (see Glossary)

Combine the water, oil, beets, liquid aminos, beef-flavored base, mushrooms, and garlic in a blender and blend until smooth and creamy. It will look like and have the texture of a strawberry smoothie. Pour it into a bowl and stir in the oat flour and flaxseed, mixing well. Mix in the vital wheat gluten and knead for about 30 seconds to form a ball.

Tear off 2-inch chunks and place them in a steamer. Steam for 10 to 12 minutes, until the outside is brown. Cut into a chunk to confirm that it is beginning to turn brown along the edges but most of the inside is still pink. Transfer to a food processor and pulse until ground. It should hold together if squeezed and formed into a ball. If it does not, it was overcooked but can still be used as a ground beef substitute in sauces, enchiladas, and so on—just not meatballs or burgers.

You can refrigerate this for up to 1 week or freeze for several months.

Gluten- and Oil-Free Ground Beef Crumbles

Makes 12 ounces

I wanted to create a truly healthy ground beef substitute that was made from the least processed whole-food ingredients and that was gluten- and oil-free. If you are looking for something super clean but tasty, this is a great option. Don't expect it to taste like Beyond Meat, but it is meaty and works great for tacos, pasta sauces, and Asian dishes. Add it toward the end of whatever you are cooking, and don't simmer it in sauces for more than a few minutes in order to maintain its texture.

Olive oil (optional) for oiling the sheet pan

10 ounces king trumpet mushrooms

1 cup raw walnuts

1 cup cooked chickpeas, rinsed

½ cup rolled oats or steel-cut oats

2 tablespoons soy sauce, tamari, or Bragg Liquid Aminos (see Glossary)

1 tablespoon vegan beef base, such as Better Than Bouillon

1 teaspoon garlic powder

Preheat the oven to 350°F. Line a sheet pan with parchment paper or oil it well.

Pulse the mushrooms in a food processor until chopped into little bits, but do not process too long or it will turn to a puree. Transfer to a large bowl and set aside. Next, put the walnuts into the food processor and pulse until they are finely chopped. Transfer them to the bowl with the mushrooms. Next, pulse the chickpeas in the food processor until they are finely chopped but not completely pureed, and add them to the bowl with the mushrooms and walnuts. Finally, pulse the oats to break them down and add them to the bowl. Add the soy sauce, vegan beef base, and garlic powder to the bowl and mix everything well. Spread out on the prepared sheet pan and bake for 20 minutes. Take the pan out of the oven and break up the mixture with a wooden spoon or spatula into crumbles. Put it back in the oven and bake for another 20 minutes, or until chewy but not dry. You can use it right away, refrigerate for up to 1 week, or freeze for up to 3 months (thaw before using).

Instant Burger, Patty, Meatball, and Crumbles Mix

Makes about 3 cups mix

This instant dinner solution is a dry mix made of whole grains and legumes that you simply mix with hot water and seasonings to make burgers, sausage patties, meatballs, or crumbles. I've kept the base plain so that you can dress it up as you like with your choice of seasonings and additions, and then you will be ready to take off with your personal creative spin to turn it into crumbles for tacos, sausages for breakfast, or burgers for the grill. I've made some suggestions below for how to use it. Keep it simple, or have fun with it!

1 cup red lentils (use only red lentils, which rehydrate and cook faster than other varieties)

1 cup bulgur wheat or brown rice

½ cup raw pecans

1 tablespoon granulated garlic

½ cup dehydrated onion, or an additional 2 tablespoons granulated garlic

½ cup nutritional yeast (see Glossary)

¼ cup flaxseed or chia seeds

2 teaspoons sea salt

2 teaspoons xanthan gum (see Note)

1 teaspoon freshly ground black pepper

Combine all of the ingredients in a blender and blend until everything has been reduced to a gritty, sandy texture. Don't overblend to the point that it becomes smooth like flour; it should retain some grittiness like polenta. Store the mix in a jar in the pantry for up to 2 months or in the refrigerator for up to 6 months.

To make basic burgers, sausage patties, and crumbles:
For each cup of mix, use about ¾ cup boiling water or stock. Put the mix in a bowl. Add seasonings as desired—Italian herbs, chili powder, cumin, sausage spices, or taco seasonings. Pour the boiling water over the mixture and stir well. Cover the bowl with a lid or plate and let it sit for about 15 minutes, until the liquid is wholly absorbed. The mixture will be gooey. Now you're ready to turn it into dinner. To form burgers or sausage patties, simply shape them with your hands as desired and cook in an oiled skillet on both sides until firm. Once fully cooked, they will hold up to reheating on the grill for a barbecue. To form basic crumbles, heat about 2 tablespoons oil, any kind, in a nonstick skillet. Cook the mixture over low heat, stirring and breaking it up with a spatula for about 10 minutes, until the mixture congeals into small pieces. At first it will seem impossible that the gooey mixture will eventually congeal into crumbles, but it will.

To make meatballs (serves 4):
Preheat the oven to 350°F. Rehydrate 1 cup of the dry mix by combining it with ¾ cup hot water in a large bowl. In a food processor, pulse 4 ounces (1½ cups) white or cremini mushrooms until they are finely chopped but not pureed. Add them to the bowl with the mix. Then add 1½ cups soft breadcrumbs, 3 tablespoons tomato paste, 1 tablespoon chopped garlic, 2 teaspoons dried basil, 1 teaspoon dried rosemary, and ½ teaspoon marjoram (or just add a tablespoon of Italian herb mix in place of the basil, rosemary, and marjoram) and mix well. Season with sea salt and freshly ground black pepper. Form the mixture into 1-inch or larger balls and bake on a greased sheet pan for about 25 minutes, until firm.

To make Cheesy Smoky Burgers (serves 4):
Rehydrate 1 cup of the dry mix by combining it with ¾ cup hot water in a large bowl. In a food processor, pulse 4 ounces (1½ cups) white or cremini mushrooms until they are finely chopped but not pureed. Add them to the bowl with the mix, then stir in. Add about 6 ounces grated or crumbled vegan smoked mozzarella or other smoked cheese (such as Gouda) and 3 tablespoons of your favorite barbecue sauce. Mix well. Form into burger patties and heat 1 to 2 tablespoons neutral oil in a skillet over medium heat. Cook the patties until browned on both sides, about 3 minutes per side.

Note: Xanthan gum is a natural by-product of fermenting sugar with a particular bacteria called *Xanthomonas campestris*. It can help hold ingredients together in lieu of an egg or other coagulants. It is available at natural food stores and online.

Chinese Tender Pork

Makes about 1½ pounds

This traditional Buddhist method for making "pork" is popular throughout parts of Asia. I had the most delicious pork and noodle dish in Vietnam that featured this style of preparation. This can be used in a variety of dishes, such as in stir-fries or soups, as a topping for bowls, or in pot stickers (see Pork, Green Onion, and Shiitake Pot Stickers, page 27). The initial deep-frying of the raw seitan dough, followed by simmering, creates a uniquely fatty texture. You will want to start with a very soft dough to ensure a tender texture.

1 cup water

1 cup plus 2 tablespoons vital wheat gluten (see Glossary)

Neutral oil for frying, such as sunflower, canola, grapeseed, or avocado

3 cups vegetable broth

1 tablespoon sugar

2 tablespoons soy sauce or tamari

½ teaspoon liquid smoke (optional)

Pour the water into a medium bowl. Using a rubber spatula or wooden spoon, mix in the wheat gluten to make a soft dough.

Pour oil into a deep fryer, wok, or pot to a depth of at least 2 inches and heat to 375°F, or until a tiny bit of dough dropped into the oil rises steadily and quickly to the surface. Tear off tablespoon-size bits of dough and stretch it with your hands to flatten it as much as you can—they should be thin. They can be uneven in shape. Drop them into the oil. They will puff up and brown like a fritter, about 2 minutes. Flip to cook the other side for another minute. When browned and puffy, remove with a slotted spoon and drain on paper towels.

Meanwhile, bring the broth, sugar, and soy sauce to a boil in a saucepan over high heat then turn down to a low simmer. Add the fried pork pieces, cover, and simmer over medium-low heat for about 30 minutes, until the liquid has reduced to about a third and the pork is tender and juicy. Chinese Tender Pork can be refrigerated in its cooking broth for a week, or frozen for up to 3 months (defrost before using).

Pork Tenderlove

Makes about 2½ pounds

I have a special place in my heart for pigs (well, all animals). But a pork chop was the last piece of meat I looked at when I made the decision to become a vegetarian at the age of twelve. I *so* looked forward to that pork chop after a school camping trip where I had endured a few days of bland vegetarian food. But when my mother put my favorite meat in front of me, I suddenly made a connection and pushed it away. I never looked back. Pork was no longer food to me. It was a piggy—just like Goober (see page 74) and Oliver (see below).

While I can't say that I truly remember the flavor of pork, I do remember what I liked about it. It was tender, savory, full of umami, and *fatty*. I think that's really what any of us want when we eat a meat alternative—something that has the qualities of meat without being meat. I believe that this recipe truly does. It took me over a dozen tries to get it right, but this version of "pork" is succulent, juicy, full of umami, and highly versatile. Try it in the amazing Mustard-Glazed Pork Tenderlove with Root Vegetable Puree and Garlic Beans (page 136); Pork Tenderlove Stuffed with Onions, Leeks, and Apples (page 138); or Tonkatsu (page 70), or come up with your own special dishes.

Meet the Animals

Oliver, an auburn pig, arrived at Rancho Compasión weighing just thirty-five pounds, a little rascal who escaped the fate of being a suckling pig (his siblings all went to slaughter). When he was small, he'd come in the house and occupy the dog bed while our dogs looked on unhappily. He'd go on hikes through the hills with the dogs and run when they ran. Unfortunately, just a short year after his arrival, weighing in at close to seven hundred pounds, Oliver suffered a severe bone infection that led to his passing. He was not only the biggest in body but the biggest in personality, bringing a smile to everyone he came in contact with. At his memorial service, there was not a dry eye to be seen—he had touched so many hearts with his goofiness, love, and spirit.

RECIPE CONTINUES ➻

PORK

8 ounces oyster mushrooms

½ cup water

¼ cup neutral oil, such as sunflower, canola, avocado, or grapeseed

1 tablespoon Bragg Liquid Aminos (see Glossary) or soy sauce

1 tablespoon onion powder

1 teaspoon liquid smoke (optional)

½ teaspoon sea salt

1¾ cups vital wheat gluten (see Glossary)

½ cup unsweetened pea protein powder (see Glossary)

COOKING LIQUID

1 cup vegetable stock

½ cup neutral oil, such as sunflower, canola, avocado, or grapeseed

2 tablespoons Bragg Liquid Aminos

1 teaspoon sugar

Preheat the oven to 350°F.

Make the pork: In a food processor, combine the oyster mushrooms, water, oil, liquid aminos, onion powder, liquid smoke, and salt and process until a rough slurry is formed. It should have a rough texture; don't overprocess or it will be too smooth. Transfer to a bowl and add 1½ cups of the wheat gluten; mix well. Mix in the pea protein and knead until it starts to get firm, then add the remaining ¼ cup wheat gluten and knead into the dough until no dry patches remain. Form as you desire—for chops, divide it into 4 to 6 pieces, then pat down to form chops, or make one large loaf.

In a Dutch oven or deep baking dish, make the cooking liquid: Pour in the stock, oil, liquid aminos, and sugar. Place the loaf in it and cover the pot with a lid. Bake for 40 to 60 minutes, depending on size, flipping it every 20 minutes or so. There should be some liquid left in the dish, so pull it out before it is completely dry. Use immediately, refrigerate for up to 1 week, or freeze for several months and thaw before using.

BBQ Stick-to-Your-Ribs with Pineapple Barbecue Sauce

Serves 6

These irresistible ribs are gluten-free and made from yuba sticks, a form of dried yuba (the skin that forms on soy milk when heated), which are available at Asian grocery stores and online. If you were to stumble upon them, you would likely wonder at their strange appearance, which is somewhat like foot-long sticks of yellow crumbled paper. When they are soaked, they become pliable, and when baked, chewy like meat. Simply tossed in barbecue sauce and thrown in the oven, they make convincing ribs without a lot of work at all.

To make the ribs, you'll have to start a day before you plan to serve them, as the "yuba sticks" need to soak for 24 hours or so. But that's it: All you need to do is put them in a deep bath of water. For the barbecue sauce, I've added some tropical flair with a bit of zesty pineapple, but you can substitute any store-bought variety of barbecue sauce you like. These are tasty even at room temperature, so take them along on a picnic (just make sure you have plenty of napkins!).

1 pound dried bean curd sticks or yuba sticks (see Glossary)

1½ cups chopped fresh pineapple

1 cup tomato paste

¾ cup water

3 tablespoons soy sauce or tamari

3 tablespoons apple cider vinegar or balsamic vinegar, or combination

2 tablespoons brown sugar

2 tablespoons chipotles in adobo sauce

2 tablespoons tamarind paste or concentrate

6 cloves garlic, peeled

1 teaspoon smoked paprika (if you like heat, used hot smoked paprika)

1 teaspoon ground cumin

⅓ to ½ cup olive oil

The day before, place the yuba sticks in a large rectangular pan or dish deep enough to accommodate the contents of the package and cover them completely with water. Cover the container and let soak in the refrigerator or a cool part of your kitchen for 12 to 24 hours. They will initially float, but as they soak up the water, they will become immersed. Soaking in hot water will expedite this and your ribs will be ready in 12 hours or less; with cold water it will take up to 24 hours.

The barbecue sauce can be made anytime—the day of, the day before, a week in advance. To make it, combine the pineapple, tomato paste, water, soy sauce, vinegar, sugar, chipotles, tamarind, garlic, smoked paprika, and cumin in a blender and blend until smooth. This will make almost 4 cups, a bit more than you need for the recipe; store it in a glass jar in the refrigerator and use for other occasions.

When you are ready to bake, preheat the oven to 400°F. Line a sheet pan (or two) with parchment paper. Coat with the olive oil.

Drain the water from the yuba sticks. Toss the yuba sticks in the barbecue sauce so that they are well coated. Spread them on the prepared sheet pan(s) and toss gently to coat them with the oil on the pan. Bake for 30 minutes, or until browned or even blackened in parts. Toss with extra barbecue sauce and serve. They are excellent the next day as well.

King Trumpet Mushroom Pulled Pork

Makes about 12 ounces

Jackfruit is all the rage for vegan pulled pork, but I prefer these mushrooms. While having a more delicate texture than actual meat or other meat substitutes, this smoky, succulent concoction works beautifully in a variety of dishes, such as tacos, enchiladas, or sandwiches, or tossed with pasta or rice, or as the star of the King Trumpet Mushroom Carnitas Tacos (page 98) or King Trumpet Pulled Pork and Leek Croquettes (page 127).

1 pound king trumpet mushrooms

3 tablespoons soy sauce or tamari

2 tablespoons olive oil

1 tablespoon maple syrup

1 teaspoon smoked paprika (or use a smoker; see Variation)

Oil for sautéing, such as olive, sunflower, canola, avocado, or grapeseed

Using the tines of a fork, pull the fork down the length of the mushrooms to shred them. Whisk the soy sauce, olive oil, maple syrup, and smoked paprika in a bowl. Add the mushrooms and toss well to coat. Marinate for about 10 minutes before cooking.

To cook, heat a tablespoon or two of oil in a sauté pan and sauté the mushrooms until browned, about 5 minutes. Use immediately or store for up to 3 days in the refrigerator and reheat.

Variation

Stovetop Smoker Pulled Pork: Follow the instructions above but omit the smoked paprika. Put the mushrooms in the tray of the smoker and follow the manufacturer's instructions for the amount of wood chips to put in. Smoke for about 10 minutes, then turn off the heat and allow it to sit in the smoke for an additional 15 minutes. You can eat it as is, or cook it in a couple tablespoons of oil in a skillet until browned and a little crispy.

King Trumpet Mushroom Bacon

Makes 8 ounces

For all the bacon lovers who say they could never give up bacon, well, you needn't. King trumpet mushrooms lend a fatty, silky texture as well as chew that is reminiscent of bacon. If you are in a hurry, you can just pan-fry these in a skillet, but they become chewier when baked. Whether in a BLT or served alongside a vegan egg scramble, they will satisfy your most stubborn bacon-loving friends. While these can play a role in multiple dishes here, including the Buffalo NotCobb Salad (page 33) and Blasted Brussels Sprouts with Balsamic and Bacon (page 34), they are equally delicious skewered and served as an appetizer.

8 ounces king trumpet mushrooms (choose the largest you can find)

2 tablespoons oil, such as olive, sunflower, canola, avocado, or grapeseed, plus more for oiling the sheet pan

2 tablespoons nutritional yeast (see Glossary)

1½ tablespoon soy sauce, tamari, or Bragg Liquid Aminos (see Glossary)

1 teaspoon liquid smoke

1 tablespoon maple syrup (optional, for Canadian-style bacon)

Slice the mushrooms lengthwise into ¼-inch slices. In a bowl, combine the oil, nutritional yeast, soy sauce, and liquid smoke. For Canadian-style bacon, add the maple syrup. Toss the mushroom slices in the mixture and allow to marinate for about 30 minutes. Although they will look dry at first, the mushrooms will release their juices and be sitting in a marinade within 10 to 15 minutes.

Preheat the oven to 400°F. Oil a sheet pan.

Place the slices on the prepared sheet pan, making sure they do not overlap. Bake for about 20 minutes, then flip and bake for an additional 15 to 20 minutes, until browned. These are best enjoyed immediately, although they can be refrigerated for a few days and added cold to salads and sandwiches.

Variation

Stovetop Smoker Bacon: If you've taken my advice in the Pancetta or Smoked Tofu recipe (page 208) and invested in an inexpensive stovetop smoker (around $50), try it this way. Make the marinade as above but skip the liquid smoke. Marinate the mushrooms for at least 30 minutes or up to a couple of days if desired. Then smoke in your smoker for about 20 minutes, following the manufacturer's instructions for adding wood chips and heating if necessary. You can store the bacon in the fridge for up to 1 week after smoking, until you are ready to cook and serve. To cook, sear the bacon for 2 to 3 minutes on each side in an oiled skillet until browned.

Lion's Mane Mushroom Steak

Makes 4 to 8 steaks

I love the idea of mushroom foraging, and while I have stumbled upon chanterelles in the woods on a few occasions (and lived to tell the tale), most of my mushroom hunting is at a store called the Berkeley Bowl. They have the largest selection of mushrooms imaginable, and every time I get a chance to go there, I find myself going home with exotic mushrooms the likes of which I had never seen. I remember several years ago coming home with these puffy white balls and throwing them on the grill to see how they would taste simply basted in a little olive oil with a sprinkling of salt. I marveled as I watched them shrink down and darken in color to resemble a slab of steak. They are not too dissimilar to puffballs, which also respond well to the same treatment, turning into a juicy, meaty, satisfying steak. Let's not pretend that these taste exactly like seared flesh, but I would be shocked if a meat lover didn't love these. Serve with a side of roasted rosemary potatoes and celebrate all the amazing flavors and textures of the plant kingdom.

STEAK RUB AND MUSHROOMS

2 tablespoons freshly ground black pepper

2 tablespoons olive oil, plus more for cooking

1 teaspoon garlic powder

1 teaspoon dried thyme

½ teaspoon ground sage

1½ pounds lion's mane mushrooms (4 to 8 mushrooms)

MARINADE

¼ cup olive oil

¼ cup red wine

1 tablespoon soy sauce, tamari, or Bragg Liquid Aminos (see Glossary)

1 tablespoon mirin (see Glossary)

1 teaspoon dried thyme

½ teaspoon freshly ground black pepper

2 cloves garlic, minced

2 tablespoons red beet juice for color (optional)

In a small bowl, make the rub: Mix the pepper, olive oil, garlic powder, thyme, and sage. Rub the mushrooms all over with this mixture. Heat a skillet over medium heat and brush it lightly with olive oil. Put the mushrooms in the skillet and cook until browned on the bottom. Flip the mushrooms, then use a lid to press the mushrooms down firmly to flatten. They will release a considerable amount of juice, which will evaporate in the pan. When they are browned on both sides and flattened to about half their original height, turn off the heat.

Make the marinade: Combine the olive oil, red wine, soy sauce, mirin, thyme, pepper, and garlic. Add the beet juice. Put the mushrooms in a shallow dish and pour the marinade over them. Cover and marinate in the refrigerator for at least 2 hours or up to 8 hours.

Right before you are ready to eat, heat a skillet and add a tablespoon or so of olive oil. Remove the mushrooms from the marinade and sear them over high heat on both sides for 3 to 4 minutes until browned. Serve immediately.

Prosciutto

Makes up to 50 sheets

This is a pretty remarkable rendition that can wrap around asparagus or melon, or serve as a filling for a sandwich. Because it's made of rice paper, it will dissolve in liquids, so it's not something that will work in soup. It makes a lovely wrapping for Pork Tenderlove Stuffed with Onions, Leeks, and Apples (page 138).

About ⅓ cup olive oil

¼ cup beet juice, or 2 thin slices red beets for color

1 cup vegetable broth

¼ cup Bragg Liquid Aminos (see Glossary)

2 teaspoons sugar

2 teaspoons liquid smoke

Up to 50 sheets rice paper (see Glossary; 1 sheet makes 1 slice of Prosciutto)

Have the oil ready in a small bowl.

If you are using beet juice, mix it with the broth, liquid aminos, sugar, and liquid smoke in a bowl or measuring cup. If you are using sliced beets, put them with the broth, liquid aminos, sugar, and liquid smoke in a blender and blend until no beet pieces remain. If your blender isn't high speed enough to render a liquid without beet bits, strain it through a sieve. Pour this liquid into a 9-inch round baking dish or cake pan. Put 3 or 4 sheets of the rice paper in the marinade and allow it to marinate for 2 to 3 minutes, until soft. Remove one sheet at a time and generously coat the rice papers on both sides with oil using your hands. The oil prevents them from sticking to each other. Once oiled properly, you can fold them in half and stack all of the sheets, and they won't stick to each other. Repeat with the remaining sheets.

This marinade is enough for up to about 50 sheets. You likely won't make that many, but it doesn't work to make a smaller amount of the marinade, as it won't be deep enough in the dish to soak, so you'll have to make this amount.

The Prosciutto will keep, tightly covered in the refrigerator, for up to 1 week.

Variation

Prosciutto-Wrapped Melon and Basil: Okay, so let's go there. The traditional prosciutto-wrapped melon is better with a small leaf of basil. Slice melon about ¼ inch thick, place a small basil leaf on top, and wrap with a half-sheet of Prosciutto. Instant appetizer, and so simple.

Pancetta or Smoked Tofu

Makes 12 ounces

Pancetta, the salty, smoky, dense cured pork that is the star of Moon Carbonara (page 176) and other dishes, is often replicated in Italy by high-quality smoked tofu. Unfortunately, I have not been able to find any commercial smoked tofu in the United States that comes close to what I had in Italy. I don't know if it's because our love for expedience leads American tofu manufacturers to rely on liquid smoke rather than actually using a smoker. So, I say—get thee to a kitchenware store and buy a stovetop smoker! I know—there is no end to the number of kitchen appliances and gadgets we can buy, with many or most of them taking up full-time residence in a dusty corner of a drawer to be used once then forgotten. But if smoky things are *your* thing, then do me a favor and spend fifty bucks on a stovetop smoker. All the liquid smoke in the world cannot do vegan pancetta, pulled pork, or a host of other dishes justice. There. I've had my say. But assuming that most people don't have a smoker, I've provided instructions for making this in the oven with liquid smoke.

Meet the Animals

What is pork belly good for? To some, it's pancetta. To me, it's for giving belly rubs. Next to eating, a belly rub is the favorite activity for piggies big and small. Whether it's our pot-bellies or our large farm pigs, they love nothing more than to flop down and have you massage their bellies. You should see the smiles on their faces! May all pig bellies be left for rubbing, not eating!

1 pound extra-firm tofu, the kind in a vacuum-packed bag (not the plastic tub with water)

¼ cup Bragg Liquid Aminos (see Glossary) or soy sauce

3 tablespoons toasted pumpkin seed oil (preferred) or olive oil

1 teaspoon sugar or maple syrup

2 teaspoons liquid smoke (if using an oven instead of a smoker)

Slice the tofu ½ inch thick. Place all of the slices on paper towels several layers thick, then top with more paper towels. Place a heavy weight—a pot with water or something—and let sit for 30 minutes or longer. Change the paper towels and repeat for another 30 minutes. The tofu must be very firm.

In a shallow dish, combine the liquid aminos, pumpkin seed oil, and sugar; if you are going to bake rather than smoke your tofu, add the liquid smoke. Put the tofu slices in the mixture and turn over to coat, then marinate for at least 3 hours or up to 24 hours.

Smoker method:

Prepare your smoker by following the manufacturer's instructions for placing wood chips in the bottom. There is usually a metal dish that comes with the smoker. Brush it with oil. Place the tofu slices in the dish and pour the remaining marinade over it. Cover the smoker, turn the heat to low, and smoke for about 45 minutes, until the tofu is smoky and very brown.

Oven method:

Preheat the oven to 300°F. Put the tofu in a shallow baking dish that will hold the slices in one layer and pour any residual marinade over it. Cover the dish with aluminum foil. Bake for 1 hour, then flip the slices and bake for an additional hour, for a total of 2 hours. The tofu should be very brown and dense.

You can store this refrigerated for a week.

Juicy Chicken

Makes 12 breasts or 1 large chicken for rotisserie, about 3 pounds

This started out as adaptation of my versatile Breast of UnChicken from *The Homemade Vegan Pantry* but took a couple of turns for the better after I found some new inspiration midstream, including the second method that resulted from discovering that I was lacking some ingredients after I'd already started (now you know how prepared I always am!). In my original recipe from *The Homemade Vegan Pantry*, the chicken breasts are wrapped in yuba (sometimes known as tofu skin) to form a succulent and tasty skin. In this recipe, I decided to add the yuba into the meat mixture, which helped create a meatier, flakier texture that was not one solid mass like most seitan recipes. The second improvement came about when I was measuring the wheat gluten and realized I was short a whole cup. So I substituted part of it with pea protein. This created an even better texture, although the first was delicious as well. Make it either way—you won't be disappointed.

Juicy Chicken plays a star role in Colonel Compassion's Best-Ever Buttermilk Fried Chicken (page 46). It is magnificent for Rotisserie Chicken (page 52), especially since there isn't anything else on the market yet that is a nice, large, whole chicken. And while there are a few "chicken breasts" out there, Chicken Breast Stuffed with Butternut Squash and Champagne Pomegranate Sauce (page 116) is better with this.

1 pound medium or medium-firm tofu

⅓ cup plus 3 tablespoons neutral oil, such as sunflower, canola, avocado, or grapeseed

⅓ cup water

⅓ cup nutritional yeast (see Glossary)

2 tablespoons vegan chicken base, such as Better Than Bouillon, vegan chicken broth powder, or 4 vegan chicken bouillon cubes (if using bouillon cubes, dissolve in the water above first)

1 tablespoon onion powder

1 tablespoon garlic powder

6 ounces frozen yuba, or 8 ounces fresh yuba (see Glossary)

3 cups vital wheat gluten, or 2 cups vital wheat gluten and ¾ cup unsweetened pea protein powder (see Glossary)

About 4 cups vegan chicken broth, such as Better Than Bouillon

2 tablespoons soy sauce or tamari

In a food processor, combine the tofu, ⅓ cup of the oil, the water, nutritional yeast, chicken base, onion powder, and garlic powder and process until smooth. If the yuba is frozen, soak in a bowl of water for 2 to 5 minutes, until it softens and turns whiter in color, then remove it and gently squeeze out the excess soaking water. If the yuba is fresh, you do not need to soak it. Roughly tear the yuba with your hands and add to the food processor. Pulse for a few seconds, until the yuba is chopped up into large, flaky bits, but do not overprocess or it will become mush. Transfer to a bowl and mix in the wheat gluten. On a clean surface, knead the mixture for 5 to 6 minutes, until fairly firm and the whole thing can be rolled into a log about 4 inches in diameter. (You can knead it for 10 to 15 minutes if you like—the longer you knead it, the firmer it will be.)

For breasts, cut the log into 12 slices. To make a whole chicken, form as best as you can into a large oval or round.

To cook, if you are making breasts, heat the remaining 3 tablespoons of oil in a large, deep frying pan. If you are making a whole chicken, heat the oil in a heavy-bottom pot that is at least twice the size of the chicken. Add the chicken to the pan or pot and cook on both sides over medium heat until browned, 3 to 4 minutes on each side. Pour broth to cover the chicken and add the soy sauce. Cover and bring to a boil, then turn down the heat to maintain a slow simmer and cook for 30 to 60 minutes (30 minutes for slices, up to 60 minutes for a whole chicken).

The Juicy Chicken can be stored in the fridge for up to 4 days or in the freezer for up to 6 months (thaw before using).

Savory Roasted Chicken

**Makes between 1 pound 12 ounces and 2 pounds,
depending on the protein content of your flour**

I know how it is. You flip through a cookbook and get a yearning to make a recipe like Colonel Compassion's Best-Ever Buttermilk Fried Chicken (page 46) or Rotisserie Chicken (page 52). But then you check your cupboard and don't have the rarer ingredients—maybe it's the vital wheat gluten, or maybe it's the yuba, and you can't find them at your local store. So I wanted to offer one recipe using an ingredient that is ubiquitous—all-purpose flour. This is how I made my meat substitutes more than thirty years ago when vital wheat gluten wasn't even available, and the seitan recipes in my very first cookbook from 1990 featured this method. But of course, it predates me—this is how the monks and Buddhists of Asia have been making gluten or "seitan" for centuries—just out of plain flour. Yes, it takes a bit more time and muscle power, but the results are pretty darn amazing, as I discovered recently when I went back to this method after decades. I had actually forgotten how good it was, as I had become enamored with the convenience of vital wheat gluten. So now I'm resurrecting it, and I hope you'll give it a try.

This chicken is full of flavor with a great, slightly sinewy texture. Highly versatile, it can be used in any recipe that calls for chicken in this book, and is a perfect stand-in for Juicy Chicken in everything. Shape it any way you want, into "breasts," steaks, or the whole "bird" for Rotisserie Chicken.

What happens here borders on magical: You make a firm dough of flour and water, then work the dough in pots of water to wash away the starch (and bran, if you use whole wheat). At the end, you're left with a much smaller mass of stretchy stuff that is the concentrated protein. It's pretty amazing, actually. The final yield will depend on the strength of the flour, meaning its protein content. All-purpose flour will give you about a pound and 10 to 12 ounces, but using a high-protein bread flour might result in 2 pounds. Just don't use pastry flour. One more thing: Whole wheat flour works, too, giving you "dark" meat, while all-purpose will give you white.

10 cups all-purpose, whole wheat, or bread flour

About 5 cups water

3 tablespoon nutritional yeast (see Glossary)

3 tablespoons neutral oil, such as sunflower, canola, avocado, or grapeseed, plus more for baking

2 tablespoons chickpea or white miso

1 tablespoon vegan chicken base, such as Better Than Bouillon

Put the flour in a large bowl, then add 4½ cups of the water and mix well to form a stiff dough. If the dough has dry pockets, add the additional ½ cup water, a little at a time, to incorporate. The dough should be firmer than regular bread dough. Knead it for a minute or two to make it smooth, then cover the bowl with a towel and let it rest for an hour. Take a walk, play with your dogs, go do something else—the dough isn't going anywhere. Maybe don't lift weights, though, because your arms are going to be getting a bit of exercise in the next step.

When you return, transfer the dough to the largest pot or tub you can find. Fill it with water to cover and start kneading the dough in the water. The starch will begin to come out, turning the water very white. Continue doing this for a couple of minutes, then dump out the water and refill the pot with clean water. Repeat with the kneading. During the process, the dough will go through a period where it feels like it is falling apart into little bits and pieces—don't worry, it will all come back together as all of the starch washes out. When this begins to happen, drain the water through a colander to catch any loose pieces.

Continue the washing process three or four more times until the water runs fairly clear. This means that you have washed out most or all of the starch, and you should have a stretchy, cohesive mass that resembles a giant wad of chewed bubble gum. This is now referred to as raw gluten. While it can be cooked in a variety of ways, including steaming, simmering in broth, or roasting, I find that the way described here is extra tasty and versatile.

Preheat the oven to 350°F. In a food processor, combine the nutritional yeast, oil, miso, and vegan chicken base and process to make a paste. Drop the raw gluten into the food processor and pulse a few times to incorporate the paste into it. The gluten will break up some; that is okay. Remove it from the bowl of the processor, scrape out any remaining paste, and incorporate it as well as you can by hand. The mass will no longer be entirely cohesive, but it will all come back together while baking.

Now lightly oil a sheet of parchment paper, and place the mass in the middle, forming as much of a loaf as possible (to be a "whole chicken"). Wrap the parchment paper around it, then wrap the whole thing in aluminum foil. Bake the chicken for about 1 hour, until the gluten is no longer raw.

Slice it, chunk it, chop it, cut it into steaks, or use it whole for any vegan chicken recipe in this book. It can be stored in the fridge for up to 4 days or in the freezer for up to 6 months (thaw before using). Enjoy!

Chilled Ginger Yuba Chicken

Serves 4 to 6

The first part of the recipe is actually for an easy DIY chicken made from yuba, which makes it gluten-free (if you use the tamari). While this chicken can be used in other dishes, such as scallopini, it's marvelously tasty and refreshing with this cold ginger marinade, making these morsels a perfect prelude to a summer dinner or in salads or as a topping for a rice bowl.

CHICKEN

8 ounces frozen yuba (see Glossary)

6 cups vegan chicken broth, such as Better Than Bouillon

2 tablespoons soy sauce or tamari

2 tablespoons nutritional yeast (see Glossary)

MARINADE

½ cup vegan chicken broth, such as Better Than Bouillon

2 tablespoons soy sauce or tamari

2 tablespoons sake

1 clove garlic, minced

1 tablespoon grated ginger, or more to taste

TOPPINGS

¼ cup chopped green onions (white and green parts)

¼ cup chopped fresh cilantro

½ cup chopped salted roasted peanuts (optional)

Make the chicken: Soak the yuba in cold water in a shallow dish, such as a 9 by 13-inch baking dish, for 5 minutes. Drain and squeeze gently to extract the water. Unfold it into a single layer, then starting at one end, roll it up as tightly as possible. Wrap it with kitchen twine to make a nice tight log. Combine the broth, soy sauce, and nutritional yeast in a 2-quart pot and immerse the yuba log in it. Bring to a boil, turn the heat down to medium-low, and simmer for 45 to 60 minutes, until firm and the mass has congealed. Allow to cool, then remove the twine. Cut into 1-inch slices.

While the chicken is simmering, make the marinade: Combine the chicken broth, soy sauce, sake, garlic, and ginger and pour into a storage container. Place the slices of chicken in it and refrigerate for several hours, preferably overnight or up to 24 hours. Serve chilled, topped with the green onions, cilantro, and peanuts.

Oyster Mushroom Fried Chicken

Makes about 8 large pieces

This "whole foods" version of fried chicken is made from oyster mushrooms, chickpeas, and rice paper. It doesn't try to be chicken exactly but offers the same satisfaction as one of America's favorite foods. The oyster mushrooms are partially baked to render them as chewy as possible while maintaining their juiciness, then they are mixed with cooked chickpeas and seasonings. The whole thing is formed into "breasts" and wrapped in rice paper, which holds it all together. Once battered and fried, it offers the crispy-on-the-outside, juicy-on-the-inside satisfaction that people love. Make it for Sunday night and you'll see happy faces around the table.

CHICKEN

1½ pounds oyster mushrooms

2 cups cooked chickpeas

2 tablespoons nutritional yeast (see Glossary)

2 teaspoons vegan chicken base, such as Better Than Bouillon, or 1 vegan chicken bouillon cube, crushed into a powder

About 8 sheets rice paper (see Glossary)

BATTER

2 cups unsweetened plain or "original" flavor nondairy milk

2 tablespoons yellow mustard

2 cups all-purpose flour

1 tablespoon garlic powder

1 tablespoon onion powder

1 teaspoon smoked paprika

1 teaspoon sea salt

1 teaspoon freshly ground black pepper

Neutral oil for frying, such as sunflower, canola, avocado, or grapeseed

Make the chicken: Preheat the oven to 325°F. Line a sheet pan with parchment paper.

Cut the mushrooms into 1-inch pieces and place them on the prepared sheet pan. Bake for 15 to 20 minutes, until they have shrunk and dried to some degree and become somewhat chewy. They should not be completely dry. Remove from the oven.

Put the chickpeas in a bowl and mash well, preferably with an immersion blender (alternatively, this can be done in a food processor, if you don't mind washing another implement). Mix in the nutritional yeast and vegan chicken base. Add the baked mushrooms and mix well.

Dip a sheet of rice paper in a bowl of warm water, then remove it and put it on a clean surface. Let it soften a bit, which will take 30 seconds or so. Put about a rounded ½ cup of the mixture in the middle of the rice paper and fold over the sides tightly so that it forms a packet that sticks together. Repeat with the remaining sheets of rice paper and mixture and set aside.

Make the batter: Mix the milk and mustard in a measuring cup. In a bowl, combine the flour with the garlic power, onion powder, smoked paprika, salt, and pepper and whisk well to combine. Take out about ½ cup of this mixture and put it in another bowl. Make a well in the original bowl of the flour mixture, pour in the milk mixture, and mix well to form a thick batter.

Dip the chicken pieces in the batter, then coat them in the flour mixture. Put the battered and coated pieces on a plate or sheet pan lined with parchment paper. Repeat with the remaining pieces.

Pour about ½ inch of oil in a deep pan (or enough to cover the chicken halfway) and turn the heat to medium-high. Let it heat to about 350°F, or until a drop of batter dropped in rises immediately and steadily to the top. Using tongs, gently place the battered chicken in the oil and repeat with the remaining pieces, being careful not to crowd the pan. Cover the pan and cook for 3 to 4 minutes, until the bottom is golden brown, then flip and cook the other side. Remove with a slotted spoon and set on paper towels to drain. Repeat until all of the chicken pieces are cooked. Serve immediately, while hot.

Variation

Oyster Mushroom Chicken with Gravy: The leftover oil alone is quite flavorful and makes great gravy. Pour off all but about ½ cup of oil. While still hot, stir in about ⅔ cup all-purpose flour and cook for about 2 minutes, stirring with a wooden spoon. It should bubble and turn white. If it is too thick and clumpy, add a bit of oil back in; if it is too runny, add a bit more flour. This is easy, like gravy—don't sweat over exact quantities.

Now add about 3 cups hot water and stir like mad with a whisk to get out the clumps and make a smooth gravy (although you might have some fried bits and pieces in it). Season the gravy with (approximate quantities) 2 to 3 tablespoons soy sauce, tamari, or Bragg Liquid Aminos (see Glossary); 3 to 4 tablespoons nutritional yeast (see Glossary); and 1 tablespoon umami, porcini, or other mushroom powder (optional). Whisk away until smooth and serve over the chicken—and don't forget the mashed potatoes.

Homemade Ground Chicken

Makes 1¼ pounds

A slight variation on the Juicy Chicken (page 210) sans the yuba turns into a tasty "raw" ground chicken that can be used in casseroles, enchiladas, tacos, pot stickers, you name it. It's a great staple to keep in your freezer and pull out whenever you need a quick and easy protein.

8 ounces medium or medium-firm tofu

5 tablespoons neutral oil, such as sunflower, canola, avocado, or grapeseed

¼ cup water

3 tablespoons nutritional yeast (see Glossary)

1 tablespoon vegan chicken base, such as Better Than Bouillon, vegan chicken broth powder, or 2 vegan chicken bouillon cubes (if using bouillon cubes, dissolve in the water above first)

2 teaspoons onion powder

2 teaspoons garlic powder

1½ cups vital wheat gluten (see Glossary)

In a food processor, combine the tofu, 3 tablespoons of the oil, water, nutritional yeast, chicken base, onion powder, and garlic powder and process until smooth. Add the wheat gluten and process until a ball forms in the middle of the bowl. Form into a log and cut it into 1-inch-thick slices.

Heat the remaining 2 tablespoons oil in a skillet over medium-low heat and briefly cook the slices in it, covered, until they are very light brown on both sides, 2 to 3 minutes per side. Do not allow them to get beyond a light brown color or they will become crispy, which will overcook them and render them too dry after grinding up. Remove the slices, cut or tear them into 1- or 2-inch chunks, and return to the food processor. Pulse until they are chopped up and resemble ground chicken. This chicken is only partially cooked, so it will need to undergo heat treatment, such as sautéing, baking, or frying. It can be stored in the fridge for up to 4 days or in the freezer for up to 6 months (thaw before using).

Chicken Burgers

Serves 6

Turn some or all of the ground chicken (opposite) into burgers. Because the ground chicken is not fully cooked, the gluten is still moist and sticky and will hold together when shaped into a burger. In terms of the seasonings and veggies added to this, it's a loose recipe, so use the quantities below as a guideline. You can adjust the amounts based on how much of the ground chicken you want to turn into burgers.

1 small yellow or white onion, cut into eighths

1 stalk celery, chopped roughly

1 to 2 cloves garlic, peeled

1¼ pounds Homemade Ground Chicken (opposite)

1 teaspoon poultry seasoning

1 to 2 teaspoons vegan chicken base, such as Better Than Bouillon, or 1 vegan chicken bouillon cube

Neutral oil, such as sunflower, canola, avocado, or grapeseed for cooking the burgers

In a food processor, pulse the onion, celery, and garlic until very finely minced. Put into a bowl and combine with the ground chicken, poultry seasoning, and vegan chicken base. Mix well. Form burgers, squeezing the mixture together. They should hold their shape. Pour a couple tablespoons of oil in a skillet and cook, covered, over medium-low heat for 4 to 5 minutes per side until browned on both sides.

The Unturkey

Serves 10 to 12, with leftovers

To some, this liberated bird is almost legendary. It originated over thirty-five years ago in my Tokyo apartment when I concocted a vegan turkey from gluten and yuba (the skin that forms on soy milk when you heat it) to entertain my Japanese friends who were curious about real turkey. The original recipe made from homemade gluten was published in my very first cookbook, *The Now and Zen Epicure*, before vital wheat gluten was available in stores. It was quite an ordeal, making a dough from whole wheat flour, then washing it under running water for a half hour until you were left with something that was like chewed bubble gum.

In the early 1990s, I started serving it for Thanksgiving every year at my San Francisco restaurant, Now and Zen, and then sold it nationwide as a competitor to Tofurky for a decade or so. Even now, people ask me if I am going to make and sell it again. The company that bought my business eventually went out of business . . . and with that, the Unturkey flew the coop and was no more. But then a fan resurrected it as a website, unturkey.org, sharing the story and the recipe for all those whose Thanksgivings wouldn't be the same without it. Eventually, I posted a video of it on YouTube, which still gets many views each season.

The Unturkey is a big bird, fully stuffed, with a crispy, tasty skin. The seitan is tender and juicy, and the cooking liquid is the base for a delicious gravy. It embodies the full experience of the Thanksgiving table, including those precious leftovers that can be turned into Unturkey noodle soup, shepherd's pie (top it with leftover mashed potatoes), or just some good ol' Unturkey sandwiches. I mean, what's Thanksgiving without leftovers?

It's a big recipe with several parts—the seitan, the all-important seasoning, the stuffing, and the gravy. Before you make anything, *make the seasoning first*. And fear not this great unbird—there are multiple steps, but all doable. If you want, you can make parts or all of it the weekend ahead of Thanksgiving (or even *weeks* ahead) and freeze it, then just reheat it on the big day. I've provided a step-by-step synopsis so you can get a sense of the flow. If you decide to make the whole shebang days, weeks, or even months ahead, please remember that it will take up to 36 hours for it to thaw in the

RECIPE CONTINUES ➻

refrigerator. This does make Thanksgiving day preparation easier, however, as all you have to do is pop it in the oven, baste it a couple of times, and make the gravy. I typically make it a couple of weekends in advance when it's not so hectic and freeze it, leaving me plenty of time on Thanksgiving Day to focus on the mashed potatoes and other sides.

Step 1   Make the seasoning (5 minutes)—this can be done months ahead and stored in the pantry.

Step 2   Mix and cook the seitan "bird" (10 minutes to mix, 1 hour to cook)—you will need about 1 yard of cheesecloth for this step. It can be made either 1 day or up to 3 months ahead and stored refrigerated (for up to 36 hours) or frozen (for up to 3 months).

Step 3   While the seitan is simmering, start making the stuffing (20 minutes to prep the veggies and bread, then mix)—you can make and stuff the Unturkey a day or up to 3 months ahead (if you are making this more than a couple of days in advance, please wrap well and freeze).

Step 4   Prepare the yuba "skin" right before you are ready to assemble the bird (5 minutes). Do the "day of" or, as part of a "make ahead," a day before or up to 3 months ahead and frozen.

Step 5   Stuff the unbird with the stuffing and enrobe in the "skin" (15 minutes). Do the "day of" or day before (or you can do this up to 3 months ahead—you will need to wrap it well and freeze).

Step 6   Bake the Unturkey, basting with the basting liquid a couple of times (60 to 90 minutes before serving).

Step 7   While baking, make the gravy (10 minutes)—best to make this the "day of" from the thawed cooking liquid.

Step 8   Eat! (who knows how many minutes?!)

Step 1 Make the Unturkey Seasoning

Makes about 2 cups

This is a pretty darn tasty instant broth and seasoning. Make a double batch and keep it in your cupboard for other dishes. It can be made well in advance—even months.

2 cups nutritional yeast (see Glossary)

2 tablespoons sea salt

2 tablespoons garlic powder

2 tablespoons onion powder

2 tablespoons dried thyme

2 tablespoons celery seed

2 tablespoons rubbed sage

2 teaspoons dried rosemary

2 teaspoons paprika

2 teaspoons dried tarragon

2 teaspoons dried marjoram

2 teaspoons freshly ground black pepper

1 teaspoon ground turmeric

1 teaspoon ground ginger

Combine all the ingredients in a blender and blend until pulverized. Transfer to a jar, where it will keep in your cupboard for up to 3 months.

Step 2 Make the "Bird" and Unturkey Broth

6 cups water, plus 1 gallon

1½ cups Unturkey Seasoning (see above)

8 cups vital wheat gluten (see Glossary)

⅓ cup soy sauce or tamari

Pour 6 cups of water into a large bowl, then whisk in ½ cup of the Unturkey Seasoning. Using a wooden spoon, mix in the wheat gluten, 1 to 2 cups at a time, until you have a rather soft dough. You don't need to knead it, unless you like a firm seitan—the idea is to render a tender "meat" that soaks up juices as it cooks.

Spread about 1 yard of cheesecloth on a clean counter or cutting board. Pat the dough into a rectangle 14 to 15 inches long and about 10 inches wide. Fold the cheesecloth over the seitan, then roll it up loosely. Using kitchen twine, tie up the roll so that it stays together. It doesn't have to be very tight, as it will expand while simmering.

Now place the seitan into a pot and pour the remaining gallon of water over it. Add the remaining 1 cup seasoning and the soy sauce. Partially cover and bring to a boil, then turn the heat down so that it is just above a simmer and cook for 1¼ to 1½ hours. To check for doneness, slice into

RECIPE CONTINUES ➤➤

the Unturkey and ensure that it doesn't look rubbery like raw gluten—there should be a consistent color and small air pockets. At this point, you will probably want to let it cool in the pot before handling, so turn your attention to making the stuffing. Don't discard the cooking liquid (now Unturkey Broth), as you'll need it for both the stuffing and the gravy. You can make the "bird" a day or weeks in advance. Allow it to cool completely, then remove the cheesecloth and discard. Refrigerate the bird and store overnight in the cooking liquid, or freeze the bird and the cooking liquid separately for more than 2 days or up to 3 months.

Step 3 Make the Stuffing

½ cup vegan butter, such as Miyoko's, or neutral oil, such as sunflower, canola, avocado, or grapeseed

1 large or 2 medium yellow or white onions, diced

4 stalks celery, sliced

3 carrots, diced

8 ounces white or cremini mushrooms, sliced

1 teaspoon plus a pinch of sea salt

1½ pounds toasted cubed bread or croutons (use stale baguettes if you have any—I always seem to have dried bread leftover from parties)

1 tablespoon dried rubbed sage

2 teaspoon dried thyme

1½ teaspoons dried marjoram

1 cup or more Unturkey Broth (page 223) to moisten

In a large, deep pan, melt the butter over medium heat. Add the onions, celery, carrots, mushrooms, and a good pinch of salt and sauté over medium heat to wilt the vegetables, about 3 minutes (they do not have to be completely tender). Turn off the heat and mix in the cubed bread or croutons, the sage, thyme, marjoram, and the remaining 1 teaspoon salt and mix well. Pour 1 cup of the Unturkey Broth over the whole thing and mix well to ensure moistness. If it is a tad dry, add more Unturkey Broth.

Step 4 Prepare the Yuba Skin

Keep in mind that this step should only be done minutes before you stuff and bake the Unturkey, unless you did it days, weeks, or months in advance and had it well-wrapped and frozen. If you are not going to stuff and bake it for a while, do not proceed with preparing the yuba skin.

3 large sheets frozen yuba, thawed (see Glossary)

½ cup white wine
½ cup olive oil

3 tablespoons Unturkey Seasoning (see page 223)

Run the yuba under warm water for a few seconds to get it wet. Let it sit for about 5 minutes. It will become lighter in color, soft, and pliable. Gently squeeze the yuba to extract the water. Make the basting liquid: In a bowl, whisk together the white wine, olive oil, and Unturkey Seasoning. Dip each piece of yuba in this mixture and use your hands to ensure that each sheet is covered in this basting liquid. If the yuba is soaking in it, squeeze it gently back into the bowl.

Step 5 Stuff and Enrobe the
Bird with Skin

Now you are ready to stuff, wrap the skin, and bake the Unturkey. First, preheat the oven to 350°F. Get a large roasting pan ready by lightly greasing it with oil.

Take a sheet of the seasoned yuba and spread it out in the pan. Put the Unturkey on a cutting board and take a good look at the shape—each one will be different. Decide which side will be the top. Starting from the opposite end, split the turkey with a knife almost up to the top, but do not cut through. You should now be able to open up the Unturkey. Place a big mound of stuffing (maybe half—you can surround the Unturkey with the remaining stuffing) in the middle of the yuba sheet in the roasting pan. Take the split Unturkey and opening it up, place the two sides over the mound of stuffing. Grab the sheet of yuba and bring it up around the Unturkey. Take the other 2 sheets of yuba and cover the rest of the Unturkey, tucking it underneath to make it look neat.

RECIPE CONTINUES ➼

The Unturkey CONTINUED

Step 6 Bake and Baste!

Cover the Unturkey and roasting pan with aluminum foil and bake for about 1 hour. Take the Unturkey out of the oven, remove the aluminum foil, and baste it all over with the basting liquid using a basting brush. Put it back in the oven for another 15 minutes, or until the Unturkey is deliciously golden brown. Upon removing, baste it once again. Note: If you are making this days or weeks in advance and freezing it, bake the Unturkey for only 15 minutes, then allow to cool. Wrap well in aluminum foil and freeze. To reheat, allow it to thaw for a full 24 hours in the refrigerator, then bake for 1¼ to 1½ hours, covered with aluminum foil the entire time except for the last 15 minutes to allow it to brown.

Step 7 Make the Gravy

Makes 4½ cups

While the Unturkey is baking, make the gravy.

½ cup vegan butter, such as Miyoko's, or neutral oil, such as sunflower, canola, avocado, or grapeseed

⅔ cup all-purpose flour

4 cups hot Unturkey Broth (see page 223)

½ cup white wine

⅓ cup Unturkey Seasoning (see page 223)

3 tablespoons soy sauce or tamari, more to taste

In a large saucepan, melt the butter or heat the oil over medium heat. Add the flour and cook, stirring with a wooden spoon, for a couple of minutes to make a light roux. Add the hot Unturkey Broth and mix well with a whisk. Add the white wine, Unturkey Seasoning, and soy sauce and simmer for about 5 minutes until nice and thick.

Step 8 Carve and Serve!

Now you're ready to present your creation. Carve the Unturkey at the table to make a splashy presentation and serve it with plenty of stuffing and gravy. Happy holidays!

Loving Lobster

Makes about 1½ pounds

You can love lobster dishes without harming them with this delicious vegan version that's also full of fiber. Featuring konnyaku, or Japanese mountain yam cake, that is the basis for zero-calorie noodles that are gaining in popularity, this lobster has that springy quality reminiscent of the magnificent creatures that roam the sea—and ensures that they remain at sea to roam, where they can live for up to a hundred years if they don't end up in a pot of bisque. Use this for Lobster Thermidor (page 130) or Garlic Lobster Fettuccine (page 132).

For those who are super experimental and food science inclined—or who simply prefer to order dry ingredients online—I've included an alternate recipe for making this from konjac powder. It holds together a bit better, but the results are almost identical otherwise.

- 1 cup water
- 3 tablespoons neutral oil, such as sunflower, canola, avocado, or grapeseed
- 2 tablespoons vegan fish sauce (see Glossary), or 1 sheet nori
- 2 teaspoons sugar
- 1 teaspoon sea salt
- 1 cup unflavored soy protein powder, such as Bob's Red Mill
- 10 ounces white konnyaku, store-bought or homemade (page 229), cut into roughly 1-inch pieces

In a food processor, combine the water, oil, fish sauce, sugar, and salt. Add the soy protein powder and process until mixed thoroughly. Add the konnyaku pieces and pulse until they are broken up into little pieces—the mixture should have uniform small lumps.

Get a steamer ready. You can use a traditional bamboo steamer set over a pot of water, or create your own with a colander set above a pot of water. Line the steamer with parchment paper and make sure you have ample water in the pot below, although it should not touch the bottom of the basket or colander. Using your hands, create oblong balls about 2 inches long. You can make the pieces bigger or smaller, as you desire.

Steam the pieces for about 20 minutes. Allow to cool before handling. Loving Lobster can be stored refrigerated for up to 4 days.

RECIPE CONTINUES ➻

Variation

"Food Science Lovers" Loving Lobster: Dissolve ⅛ teaspoon pickling lime (see Glossary) in ¼ cup water and set aside. Combine 2 cups water and 1 tablespoon konjac powder (see Glossary) in a saucepan and whisk well. Bring to a boil, then turn down the heat and let it simmer for about 3 minutes, whisking gently almost constantly. Pour in the pickling lime liquid and whisk well. Continue to cook for another minute or two. Allow this mixture to cool until it is tepid enough to handle with your hands. It will be very jelly-like. Add 2 tablespoons vegan fish sauce (see Glossary), 2 teaspoons sugar, and ½ teaspoon sea salt and mix well. Finally, mix in ¾ cup soy protein powder, mixing as necessary with your hands to incorporate. Form into balls or patties and steam, following the directions on the previous page.

Homemade Konnyaku for Lobster, Calamari Fritti, and More

Makes about 1½ pounds

This is most likely the strangest recipe in the book and definitely one for those inclined to food science. If you have a deep connection to Japanese food, then you likely know what this is and might be intrigued by the opportunity to make your own. But if you aren't, you might be asking, "So, what is konnyaku?" It's a wiggly, hard, somewhat gelatinous *thing* that's made from the konjac yam, a tuber that is high in fiber and virtually absent of calories. Yes, it's almost a miracle food, and in fact, you'll sometimes see noodles made from it sold under the brand name Miracle Noodles. In block form, it's uncannily like squid and provides a sort of bouncy texture that works perfectly for lobster.

While you can buy konnyaku at just about any Asian grocery store (it's perishable, so look in the refrigerated case), it's fun to make your own from konjac powder. If you make it yourself, you can flavor it as you like with vegan fish sauce, which really makes it taste like squid. This is the answer to the perfect Calamari Fritti (page 24) and Loving Lobster (page 227), and can also be added to Bouillabaisse (page 112) as "squid."

2 cups water

⅛ teaspoon pickling lime (see Glossary)

2 tablespoons konjac powder (see Glossary)

½ teaspoon sea salt

1 tablespoon vegan fish sauce (see Glossary)

In a wide saucepan, whisk together the water and pickling lime and let it sit for 1 minute. Whisk in the konjac powder in a steady stream to prevent clumping. Place the pan over high heat and let the mixture reach a boil. It will be hard to see, as it will be very goopy, but you will be able to see large bubbles start to push their way up. Sprinkle the salt and fish sauce over it. Using a silicone spatula, very slowly fold the mixture over to stir it (I've found that folding it over with a spatula works best because it will be too thick to stir with a whisk). The mixture will be very thick, white, and goopy. Cook for about 3 minutes, then spread out in a flat dish, such as a plate or cake pan. It will harden as it cools. When hard, it can be cut into rings for Calamari Fritti or used for Loving Lobster. The konnyaku can be kept refrigerated for up to 1 week.

Quick Buttery Scallops

Makes about 1 pound, enough to serve 4 or more

Had she tried them in Wonderland, I think even Alice would have been impressed with the transformative powers of king trumpet mushrooms. While they're not particularly flavorful on their own, they're capable of taking on the flavors and textures of many other foods (and all without hallucinogenic effects, which is convenient). Try this: If you use a small knife to score the sides of large trumpet mushrooms, then cut them into fat discs, they cook up into morsels that look, act, and taste an awful lot like sea scallops, especially with a splash of vegan fish sauce. Eat them on their own, over rice with steamed vegetables, or in Linguine with Lemon-Garlic Scallops and Herbs (page 88), Bouillabaisse (page 112), or Paella with Scallops, Sausage, and Chicken (page 180). You can skip the fish sauce for a lovely simple mushroom stir-fry.

1½ pounds large king trumpet mushrooms, caps cut off where the gills start and reserved for another use

4 tablespoons vegan butter, such as Miyoko's

1½ tablespoons vegan fish sauce (see Glossary)

2 tablespoons water

Kosher salt and freshly ground black pepper

Run a small, sharp knife lengthwise down one mushroom stem, scoring it just about ⅛ inch into the mushroom. Repeat at regular intervals four more times around the stalk. (This will allow the mushroom to shrink with ragged edges as it cooks and mimic a sea scallop in texture.) Cut the scored stalks into ¾-inch-thick discs.

Heat a large skillet over medium-high heat. Add the butter. When the butter has just melted, add the scallops with one flat side down and cook until deep golden brown, 6 to 7 minutes on each side, turning halfway through once the first side has browned. Add the fish sauce and water, swirl to coat the pan, and cook for another 30 seconds or so, stirring to coat all the scallops in the sauce. Season with salt and pepper (but taste first, as fish sauces have varying levels of saltiness) and serve hot. These are best enjoyed right after cooking, although they can be reheated in other dishes. If not eating right away, store in the refrigerator for up to 4 days.

Jackfruit Fish

Makes 8 fish fillets

More and more, vegan fish substitutes are finding their way onto store shelves, but most are battered or breaded. If you are looking for an alternative that is more whole foods–based and can be used in a variety of applications, such as Bouillabaisse (page 112), try this version using jackfruit. If simmered for a good long time in a seafood-scented broth, it will overcome its fruit-like flavor and be the perfect foil for a flaky fish. And, of course, you can batter and fry, pour a pint of ale, and have yourself some Beer-Battered Fish and Chips (page 78).

1 (20-ounce) can young green jackfruit in brine (see Glossary), drained

1 cup water

1 to 2 tablespoons vegan fish sauce (see Glossary), or 1 sheet nori

6 ounces medium or firm tofu (don't use extra-firm or the kind that is vacuum packed)

1½ teaspoons konjac powder (see Glossary)

2 sheets nori (in addition to the sheet used for the jackfruit, if it was used in place of fish sauce)

Drain the jackfruit and tear it apart with your fingers to resemble pulled pork. Put the jackfruit in a small pot and add the water and fish sauce to taste or 1 sheet of nori. Cover, bring to a boil over high heat, then turn down to a simmer and cook for about 30 minutes to tenderize and flavor the jackfruit. This will overcome the fruity aspect of jackfruit and give it a fishy flavor. If you used nori instead of fish sauce, you will likely have a wet black wad in there. You can discard that, or just break it up and add it to the dish. Drain the jackfruit well.

Meanwhile, combine the tofu and konjac powder in a small food processor and process until pureed. In a bowl, combine the jackfruit and tofu mixture. Cut or tear the 2 nori sheets into 4 long pieces each. Put a pile of the jackfruit mixture, about ⅓ cup, onto half of each piece of nori, flatten it a bit to form a fillet, and fold the nori over the mixture to enclose the jackfruit in nori.

Place all 8 pieces on a sheet of parchment paper in a steamer. Cover and steam for 30 minutes, until it feels firm. Allow to cool before using; it will firm up even more. Keep refrigerated for up to 4 days or freeze for up to 3 months (thaw before using).

Homemade Paneer

Makes 10 ounces

If tofu in your vegan saag paneer just ain't cutting it for you, give this a try. Like paneer, this cheese is very hard but will soften and melt just enough when it is heated or fried. With a tad bit of tang, it's perfect for a spicy curry. Instead of using vegan chicken in Beginner's Indian Butter Chicken (page 167), you can substitute this paneer—be sure to pan-fry it with a bit of oil to brown it before you put it in the curry at the end. It is also delicious as an addition to Turkish Beef and Rice Stuffed Squash (page 170). Or try breading and frying it, then dipping it in a tamarind sauce as an appetizer.

3 cups unsweetened plain nondairy soy or almond yogurt

4 tablespoons tapioca flour (see Glossary)

½ cup water

1 tablespoon agar powder (see Glossary)

1 teaspoon sea salt

Put the yogurt in a nut milk bag or a double layer of cheesecloth and hang it from a faucet or something with a bowl underneath to allow the whey to drain off. Leave it for about 24 hours; by then it should have a very thick mixture that is less than half the original amount. It is hard to predict exactly how much you will have from the 3 cups yogurt in the beginning, as the milk solid amounts can differ depending on the yogurt. (Coconut yogurt does not really work for this.) Measure out 1 cup of this mixture, and if you have any remaining, set it aside for another use, or adjust the ratios of the other ingredients to make more of the paneer.

Mix the tapioca flour into the strained yogurt. Pour the water into a saucepan and whisk in the agar in a steady stream. When it is fully dissolved, turn the heat to low, cover the saucepan (very important!), and bring to a simmer. It will initially get very thick, cloudy, and lumpy looking, but it will thin out when it reaches the right temperature (above 200°F). You must always leave the lid on except to check the progress a couple of times—the lid helps to trap the heat in the pan and helps the agar dissolve without burning the pan. Let it simmer for about 5 minutes, until the mixture thins out some and will drip from the spatula like molten glass.

Add the yogurt-tapioca mixture and whisk fast and furiously to incorporate it into the agar. The yogurt should be at room temperature—if it is cold from the refrigerator, it could cause the agar to seize up and form hard chunks. Keep stirring, now with a rubber spatula, until it becomes very thick and goopy. Pour into a shallow container and put in the refrigerator until firm, about an hour or two. Once firm, you can cut the paneer and use in dishes like saag paneer. Store in the refrigerator for up to 3 weeks.

Easy Buffalo Mozzarella

Makes about 1 pound

This is the mozzarella that I most enjoy making and eating, although I have recipes for several. It has that lovely bouncy springiness of fresh mozzarella and is fabulous in a caprese salad or sandwich or marinated in oil and herbs, then skewered and grilled. Because it doesn't contain any oil, it's not the best cheese for melting, but it will soften when baked. Try it in the Sausage Calzones with Roasted Fennel and Preserved Lemon (page 63) or Roasted Butternut Squash, Sausage, and Mozzarella Fettuccine (page 91).

1 cup raw cashews

1 cup unsweetened plain nondairy almond, soy, or oat yogurt

1 cup water

1½ teaspoons sea salt

3 tablespoons tapioca flour (see Glossary)

1 tablespoon agar powder (see Glossary)

Put the cashews in a bowl and add enough water to cover. Soak for 3 to 8 hours, then drain, rinse, and drain again.

Combine the yogurt, cashews, ½ cup of the water, and the salt in a blender and blend until emulsified. Transfer to a container, cover loosely, and set aside for 12 to 24 hours, until slightly tangy. Whisk in the tapioca flour.

In a small saucepan with a heavy bottom (a thin pan will simply burn the agar), whisk the agar into the remaining ½ cup water. When it is fully dissolved, turn the heat to low, cover the saucepan (very important!), and bring to a simmer. It will initially get very thick, cloudy, and lumpy looking, but it will thin out when it reaches the right temperature (above 200°F). You must always leave the lid on except to check the progress a couple of times—the lid helps to trap the heat in the pan and helps the agar dissolve without burning the pan. Let it simmer for about 5 minutes, until the mixture thins out some and will drip from the spatula like molten glass. Pour the yogurt mixture into the agar and whisk well. Raise the heat to medium and cook for 2 to 3 minutes, stirring with a wooden spoon, until the mixture is smooth, glossy, and very stretchy. Taste a bit of it to ensure that there is no residual trace of starchiness to the tongue; if it is still starchy, continue to cook for another minute.

Prepare a large bowl of ice water. Using an ice cream scooper, drop balls of the cheese into the ice bath. Let sit for 20 to 30 minutes, until firm. The larger the balls, the longer they will take to set up. They are ready when they are firm enough to be sliced easily. You can store them in the refrigerator for a week as is, or for longer keeping, immerse them in olive oil or a vinaigrette for up to a month.

Homemade Hard Parmesan

Makes 12 ounces

Here's a truly hard Parmesan that grates and melts for all of your salads and Italian favorites. It uses deodorized cocoa butter, which is very hard even at room temperature (whereas coconut oil will soften). Make sure that the cocoa butter you use is food grade and deodorized or it will end up tasting like chocolate!

1 cup almond meal

½ cup pitted green olives, such as Castelvetrano

⅓ cup olive brine

¼ cup nutritional yeast (see Glossary)

¼ cup tapioca flour (see Glossary)

2 tablespoons red miso

1 teaspoon sea salt

2 tablespoons nondairy yogurt with active cultures, any kind, or 1 vegan probiotic capsule

6 ounces deodorized cocoa butter (preferably wafers)

In a blender, combine the almond meal, olives, olive brine, nutritional yeast, tapioca flour, miso, and salt and blend until fairly smooth, keeping in mind that the almond meal will leave a little texture. Add the nondairy yogurt or probiotic capsule, and process for another 5 seconds. Transfer to a clean bowl or dish, cover with a lid or plastic wrap, and set in a warm place (between 80° and 110°F) to ferment for about 24 hours, until the mixture is sharp in flavor.

Get the deodorized cocoa butter ready. If it is in wafer form, you need do nothing. If it is in large chunks, chop it into smaller pieces.

When the fermented almond mixture is to your taste in sharpness, transfer it to a saucepan. Add the cocoa butter and turn the heat to medium. Cook the mixture, stirring almost constantly with a rubber spatula, until the cocoa butter melts and is incorporated into the mixture and the whole thing starts to thicken and become glossy. Taste occasionally to ensure that the starch has fully gelatinized; if it hasn't, you'll be able to detect a starchy note. The trick is to heat it long enough to cook the starch but not so long that the oil starts to separate. If you overcook it and the oil separates, transfer it to a bowl and put it in the refrigerator for a half hour or so to cool down a bit, then blend it in the blender again until smooth. The oil should reincorporate, but it won't if it is too hot. Pour the mixture into a mold of some form—a glass bowl, a silicone mold, a plastic container—and let it cool. Refrigerate until very firm; it will keep refrigerated for up to 3 months.

Glossary

Agar Powder Agar is a tasteless seaweed with a gelling effect that can help coagulate or add firmness to liquids. While it is more brittle than gelatin, it can be combined with tapioca to produce a similar effect. It is most readily available as powder or flakes. The recipes in this book all call for powder, which is easier to use. Agar is activated by fully dissolving in a liquid and bringing it to a boil. It then starts to set as it cools down. It will retain its firmness at room temperature. You can get agar at natural food stores or online, or at Asian grocery stores (look for Telephone brand for an economical option, and make sure you choose the kind without sugar).

Black Salt (Kala Namak) Not to be confused with black lava salt (which is just salt mixed with activated charcoal), black salt, aka *kala namak,* is a salt that has been cooked in a kiln and obtains a sulfurous smell and flavor. It can enhance dishes, adding an eggy flavor to them. The eggy flavor dissipates when cooked, so should be added at the end of a cooking process. Kala namak is available in specialty stores, Indian grocers, and online.

Bragg Liquid Aminos Invented by Paul and Patricia Bragg, this cult-status condiment is made from soybeans and water using a proprietary process to create an umami-rich, meaty, and slightly smoky substitute for soy sauce and tamari. While I've used it in many recipes here either as the recommended option or an alternative to soy sauce, it does not have the right flavor for some dishes, e.g., ones that are Asian-leaning. Bragg liquid aminos is available at natural food stores and online.

Chinese Black Vinegar This dark and slightly smoky vinegar made from sorghum, barley, and peas gets its intensity from aging for several years and is often used as a dipping sauce for pot stickers. You can get Chinese black vinegar in Asian grocery stores.

Jackfruit This tropical fruit that is luscious eaten as a fruit when ripe or as a meat substitute when it is still young and green. It is available in the latter form brined in cans.

Konjac Powder Konjac powder is the ground-up root of the konjac plant, a fibrous tuber. Widely used in Asian cuisine, it is calorie-free and full of fiber. It provides a gelatinous, firm texture to foods and is the basis for vegan calamari and lobster. It's available online, as well as at some natural food stores.

Mirin This Japanese sweet sake lends umami, mellowness, sweetness, and complexity to many dishes. Choose one that is naturally fermented with just rice and koji (it will have an actual alcohol percentage), rather than "mock" mirin, which is mostly made of sugar.

Nutritional Yeast (aka nooch) This deactivated yeast comes in flake form and is not only rich in vitamins (particularly B), minerals, and protein but packs a punch in flavor. It can add both cheesy and meaty goodness to a number of recipes. Some brands of nutritional yeast are not as flavorful; look for Red Star or Bragg.

Pea Protein Powder This is a concentrated form of protein extracted from yellow peas. Look for a brand, such as Bob's Red Mill, that is extracted using a water rather than solvent process, and make sure that it is unflavored and unsweetened. It can be found in natural food stores and online.

Pickling Lime Pickling lime is a natural mineral, calcium hydroxide, often used to increase the crispness of pickles. Mrs. Wages is a brand that can be found online.

Rice Paper The wrapper for spring rolls made from rice looks like translucent paper—hence its name. While at one time it was only found in Asian grocers, these days, it is fairly ubiquitous across the country and can be found in any major supermarket or natural food store, as well as online.

Tapioca Flour Call it tapioca flour or starch; they are one and the same. It is a starch derived from the root of the cassava plant. Tapioca creates a stretchy, elastic texture that provides synergy with agar in creating the perfect texture for vegan cheese. Add too much, however, and your creation can get gummy.

Vegan Fish Sauce The number of vegan fish sauces on the market is rising, happily, although in my experience, they range quite a bit in their "fishiness." The best I've found is made by 24 Vegan, a vegan and woman-owned company. This product can enhance Spunky Pad Thai with Chicken (page 163), Quick Buttery Scallops (page 230), or wherever you want a touch of fermented fish flavor.

Vital Wheat Gluten This is the protein of the wheat with the starch and bran removed. It's an instant gluten flour that, when combined with liquids and flavorings, forms the basis for many meat alternatives. It is found in natural food stores and online.

Yuba Ever heat up dairy milk too long so that it forms a skin on top? Well, that's what yuba is, only it's the skin of soymilk. The "skin" is removed and hung up to dry slightly or completely. Not only does it create a realistic "skin" for chicken or turkey, it can help create the flakiness you want in vegan fish or chicken. You can find it fresh in some Asian or natural food stores (look for a brand called Hodo Soy) or frozen in Asian grocery stores. If you can't find it fresh or frozen, you can use the dried version, which can be found online, but take care as it is brittle. The fresh version requires no prep—simply unpack it, unfold it, and use. The frozen version will need to be soaked for 2 to 3 minutes in water, or as directed. The dried version will require soaking in water for 10 minutes to reconstitute and become pliable before you can use it. Yuba is a Japanese word, and while Japanese brands exist, I prefer to use Chinese brands, which are typically thicker and less delicate.

Acknowledgments

Seriously. I was wondering how I was going to write a book while keeping up my crazy life as the CEO of Miyoko's. I couldn't have done it, and *wouldn't* have done it, were it not for my kind and easy-going editor, Lisa Regul, who convinced me that I was the right person for the job. And then there's my agent, Sally Ekus, who was going on maternity leave but made sure I had everything in place to start the project before she went into labor. And thanks to Jess Thomson for her assistance on many of the recipes. Ah— the long process is over, and folks should understand that a book comes together not just because of the author but because of all the people who come to support it from all sides, from the photographer (the amazing Eva Kolenko), to the designer (Isabelle Gioffredi), production manager (Jane Chinn), editors, testers (thanks again, Linda Postenreider!), and finally the willing eaters—my friends and family, who once again, became the guinea pigs for night after night of meaty dishes (one of my daughters was thrilled—"I'm *so* glad you're making these protein-packed meals," she quipped).

About the Author

Miyoko Schinner is the fearless CEO/founder of Miyoko's, a food brand combining culinary traditions with food technology to revolutionize dairy by making cheese and butter without cows.

Through an innovative proprietary process that merges food science with old-world creamery methods, Schinner has successfully scaled the production of fermented cheese and cultured butter made from plants and replaced animal-dairy products on the shelves of more than twenty thousand retailers throughout the United States and Canada. The pioneer of the plant-based cheese revolution, Schinner is a passionate culinarian, former restaurateur, best-selling cookbook author, co-host of the national public television show *Vegan Mashup*, and a founding board member of the Plant Based Foods Association. Her cookbooks include *The Homemade Vegan Pantry*, *Artisan Vegan Cheese*, *Japanese Cooking*, and *The Now and Zen Epicure*. Schinner also co-founded a farmed animal sanctuary called Rancho Compasión in California that provides a home to over a hundred rescued farm animals.

Index